Pelts, Plumes, and Hides

Pelts, Plumes, and Hides
White Traders among the Seminole Indians, 1870–1930

HARRY A. KERSEY, JR.

A Florida Atlantic University Book

The University Presses of Florida
Gainesville

For
KAREN AND LAURA

Library of Congress Cataloging in Publication Data

Kersey, Harry A   1935–
    Pelts, plumes, and hides.

    "A Florida Atlantic University book."
    Bibliography: p.
    Includes index.
    1. Fur trade—Florida—History.   2. Seminole
Indians—History. I. Title.
HD9944.U46F64   381'.439   75-16137

ISBN 0-8130-0680-5
Second printing, 1980

PRINTED BY THE STORTER PRINTING COMPANY, INCORPORATED
GAINESVILLE, FLORIDA

Foreword

In January of 1900 the Right Reverend William Crane Gray, then concluding his seventh year as Episcopal Bishop of the Missionary Jurisdiction of Southern Florida, reported to the church convocation on his work to establish a mission among the Seminole Indians in the Everglades; he characterized the Indians with whom the missionaries had to deal as being "a 'remnant of a remnant' . . . difficult to reach, suspicious of, and avoiding the white man, and, mindful of past treatment, retiring before him into the fastness of the Everglades and Big Cypress Swamp." While there were certainly exceptions to this generalization, such as Seminole camps located near the frontier villages of Miami, Fort Myers, and Fort Pierce, for the most part the Seminole people had maintained an extremely tenuous contact with the ever-encroaching white settlers. In the more than four decades which had elapsed since the conclusion of the Third Seminole War of 1855–58, the Indians had kept to their camps in the virtually impenetrable interior of the Everglades; they ventured forth only to trade the products of their hunting and trapping for the food staples, guns and ammunition, and other necessities needed to sustain life in that vast, watery wilderness. From these initial contacts with white traders, as well as with the missionaries and government agents who inevitably followed in their wake, the Seminoles began to acculturate rapidly—often in ways that did not reflect Rousseau's concept of the noble savage.

The purpose of this study is to examine the nature of the Indian trade on the Florida frontier at the turn of the century, and to focus on the reciprocal economic and social relationships which developed between the trading families and their Seminole clientele. Throughout the last quarter of the nineteenth century, the people who knew the Seminoles most intimately were the traders who frequented their camps or established accessible trading posts on the periphery of their hunting grounds. Countless traders and whiskey vendors came and went among the Indians and left no tangible evidence of their transactions. What is known of the Seminole trade comes primarily from the documents and personal accounts of those families who maintained permanent trading posts and trafficked with the Seminoles on a sustained basis. Those rugged pioneers, often living under the most primitive of conditions, were the Indian's contact with the outside world, which he loathed but also needed. The trading post was his source of supplies, as well as an outlet for his pelts, plumes, and hides. The traders, in turn, were entrepreneurs who depended upon the Seminoles for those items which they sold at a profit to warehousemen in Jacksonville, Key West, and Tampa for transshipment to eastern manufacturing centers. Thus there developed a symbiotic relationship between the trader and the Indian which was firmly rooted in economic survival.

The relationships between the trading families and the Seminoles often, however, transcended the purely economic; in most instances the traders became keen observers of Indian life, and many lasting friendships were formed. The traders often learned a good bit of the Seminole languages, while Indians gleaned at least enough English to facilitate communication during trading. The homes of the traders were generally open to the Indians during their visits, particularly at those posts which were quite isolated and where any company was usually welcome. In these informal contacts the Seminoles learned of the dominant culture; the use of a sewing machine, certain methods of preparing foods, and even a very elementary bit of reading and writing of the English language were occasionally taught by the families. There were also times when the trading posts became havens for sick or injured Indians, particularly during epidemics such as measles or influenza. The Seminoles in turn helped the white families adapt to an alien environment by introducing them to the ingenious dugout canoe as a mode of travel, the multiple uses of the palmetto frond, and such delicacies as Indian pumpkin, palm bud, coontie starch, and guava syrup, as well as turtle and manatee stew. Many of the Seminoles also evidenced their affection

and respect for various traders by adopting their English surnames.
This is not to imply that all white traders in the Everglades and
Big Cypress regions were benevolent altruists who dealt with the red
man fairly and squarely; nor were all Indians trustworthy and naïve
children of the wilderness. There were traders who grossly over-
charged for their goods, underpaid the Seminoles for hides and
plumes, and sold them rotten liquor to boot! In fact, the moonshiners
were the greatest single contributors to the degradation of the Indian during this period, and were generally abhorred by honest
traders (a surprising number of whom were teetotalers) and prosecuted by U.S. Indian agents whenever possible. However, most
traders were willing to give the Indian an honest return for his
goods within the limits of their own risky margin of profit. It should
be pointed out that the market for pelts, plumes, and hides was anything but stable after 1900, and the traders were generally taking a
"businessman's risk." The workings of this volatile market will be
explored in light of available documentary evidence.

Ironically, the traders and the Seminoles began their greatest period of interaction at the very time when the South Florida frontier
was undergoing dramatic and drastic changes that would, along
with substantial shifts in the national fashion industry, end this lucrative era of trading. The accelerated draining of Florida wetlands
began in the 1880s when Hamilton Disston, the multimillionaire
Philadelphia saw manufacturer, purchased four million acres of land
from the Internal Improvement Fund, dredged drainage canals, and
opened the Kissimmee River–Lake Okeèchobee–Caloosahatchee
River region to settlement. An influx of settlers caused the first major
shift of the Seminole population southward in Florida since the Civil
War. The comprehensive and systematic drainage of the Everglades
region south of Lake Okeechobee, inaugurated by Governor N. B.
Broward in 1907, was the second great stroke against the unre-
stricted hunting and trapping economy of the Indians. As more and
more land was drained and made fit for farming, railroad and land
development companies ousted Indian families from campsites they
had occupied for years, triggering a series of land grabs and forced
dispossessions of Indians which lasted through the Florida "land
boom" of the 1920s. The net result was a steady erosion of Seminole
economic independence, with an accompanying loss of social co-
hesiveness. Ultimately, the federal government had to step in and
set aside lands to be held in trust for the Indian people. Although

the government began purchasing land for this purpose as early as the 1890s, the Seminole reservations in Florida were not opened until the 1920s and '30s. Unlike the reservations in the West where Indian tribes were herded as prisoners, the Florida lands provided a sanctuary where the Seminoles could hunt and live unmolested. More importantly, the land would provide a stable economic base for the tribe long after hunting and trapping ceased to be viable economic alternatives. Today, the thriving beef cattle herds, citrus groves, and commercial farming enterprises on the Brighton and Big Cypress reservations, as well as business and commercial development of the urban Hollywood Reservation, attest to the basic wisdom of acquiring these parcels for the Seminoles.

The definitive history of the Seminole people over the last century has yet to be written. Most of the voluminous literature on the Florida Indians has focused on the three Seminole wars, or has presented narrow-gauge anthropological studies, such as the contributions of Goggin, Spoehr, Sturtevant, and Capron, among others. Only the work of Fairbanks has attempted to present a comprehensive picture of cultural development among the Creek Indians who came into Florida during the 1700s. Unfortunately, Fairbanks' ethnohistory, a detailed and scholarly treatise compiled in conjunction with the Seminole land claims case before the U.S. Indian Claims Commission, does not cover the period following the Seminole wars. This author has attempted to lay the ground for such research in a recent study undertaken for the U.S. Department of the Interior, Bureau of Indian Affairs. However, that work is only suggestive of the directions that a more complete history of the Indian peoples since the Third Seminole War might take. The current volume is but a further expansion and elaboration of one of its major themes: the impact of traders, missionaries, and government agents in the acculturational process of the Seminoles.

In many ways this study presented special historiographical problems, not least of which was a dearth of source material specifically dealing with trade. Although the reports of Pratt and MacCauley in the 1880s offered precise, if unsubstantiated, estimates of the extent and value of the Seminole trade, this was not true of the annual reports filed by U.S. Indian agents assigned to Florida. Not until Nash's report to the U. S. Senate in 1931 was the matter of trade again discussed in detail in assessing the economic viability of the Seminoles. Neither government documents nor the periodical literature on state and local history had a great deal to yield on the subject, and most major histories of Florida mentioned the Indian trade only in passing. By and large the most useful information on both the substance and flavor of the trading period came from the surviving members of the traders' families. In most cases they generously granted interviews, opened their ledgers and other documents to inspection, and allowed the reproduction of family photograph collections. Unfortunately, many of the valuable old trading documents have been lost over the half-century since the Seminole trading ended, more often due to fire and hurricanes than to any lack of care by the owners; nevertheless, enough of these items do remain to allow the researchers to verify the general nature of the economic transactions. But the most interesting and useful sources were the people who themselves had experienced at first hand the life and times of the frontier trading post.

It is a historical tragedy that most of the Indians who were active during the peak trading days have passed on without leaving any narrative of their activities. What little is known of their role in this interaction has been imperfectly filtered through the perceptions of the traders with whom they dealt. Although they have been given a sympathetic treatment in most accounts, it is still a second-hand rendering which cannot tell us much about how the Indian viewed his social and economic contacts with the non-Indian society. Perhaps someday the growing number of young Indian scholars, working in the native tongues, will capture the true flavor of their elders' experience before it is lost forever. In the meantime, my gratitude is expressed to friends among the Seminole and Miccosukee peoples who have aided this research in so many ways.

A special debt to colleagues at several institutions who have read and commented on portions of the manuscript must also be acknowledged; these include Dr. Sam Proctor and Dr. John Mahon of the University of Florida, Professor Charlton Tebeau of the University of Miami, as well as Dr. James Nicholas, Dr. Donald Curl, and Dr. William Sears of the Florida Atlantic University faculty. It would also be remiss not to note the extraordinary service rendered by various historical societies and research libraries in this area, especially the P. K. Yonge Library of Florida History, the University of Miami Library, the University of South Florida Library, the Historical Society of Fort Lauderdale, the St. Lucie County Museum, and the Historical Association of Southern Florida. All have added immeasurably to the quality of the research effort; final responsibility for any shortcomings of the work must, of course, reside with the author.

Finally, a word of thanks is due my family, which has patiently endured my frequent absences over the past few years while working on Indian programs. My wife has borne the period of final manuscript preparation with her usual aplomb, offering pungent criticism when asked, and often wielding a practiced editing pencil. This work is dedicated to my daughters, who have already begun to appreciate the cultural uniqueness and personal warmth of Indian children; hopefully cross-cultural values will be retained throughout their lives.

Contents

1

A Remnant of a Remnant

A T THE midpoint of the nineteenth century, that portion of the Florida peninsula lying south of Lake Okeechobee was still virtually unexplored and little known to the outside world. It was a forbidding land where the sandy soil and pine forests of the southeastern coastal plain began to give way to the more exotic flora and fauna of the subtropics—the palm tree and mangrove thicket, the alligator, crocodile, and manatee, the snowy egret and anhinga, as well as countless species unknown in northern climes. The dominant feature of the terrain was the big lake itself, the largest body of fresh water lying entirely within the United States, covering some seven hundred square miles. Actually, it was a shallow catchment area which received the drainage of the Kissimmee River and its tributaries, and the overflow escaped its southern rim as if from a giant saucer. Below the lake, the fresh water entered a broad drainage basin over thirty miles wide, through which it flowed to the Gulf of Mexico some 120 miles away. Because the drop in elevation was so slight, averaging about two inches per mile, the flow of water was almost imperceptible, and the whole area appeared to be a flat, relatively treeless plain. The Seminoles named the region "Pa-hay-o-kee," or "grassy waters," but the white man has traditionally called it the Everglades.[1]

1. Charlton W. Tebeau, *Man in the Everglades*, pp. 17–27; William B. Robertson, Jr., *Everglades—The Park Story*, pp. 5–16. For firsthand accounts of travelers crossing the Everglades prior to 1900 see Alonzo Church, "A Dash through the Everglades," pp. 15–41; Mary K. Wintringham, ed., "North to South through the Glades in 1883," pp. 33–93; Hough L. Willoughby, *Across the Everglades.*

This broad expanse of sawgrass marshes and wet prairie was dotted with elevated stands of tropical hardwood forest known as hammocks. There were also "cypress heads," or ponds, where the tall, moss-festooned trees thrived, and "bayheads" of low trees in a jungle-like growth. These tree islands offered refuge and forage for animals, as well as camp sites for Indians traversing the 'glades. In all but the driest years, the area was navigable by shallow-draft canoes which were poled along "trails" through the sawgrass. Along the east coast, this shallow inland river was separated from the Atlantic Ocean by a coastal ridge surmounted with pine forest and scrub growth. The ridge was breached in places by swift-flowing streams such as the Miami River and the New River, which formed natural avenues of transportation into the interior. On the west coast, a similar though less well defined ridge channeled the water through the Big Cypress Swamp until it ultimately merged with the brackish waters and mangrove islands that formed the shoreline of the Ten Thousand Islands.

This vast, watery wilderness was the habitat of the Indian bands which had migrated to the region during the Second Seminole War (1835–42).[2] Many of them initially remained within the boundaries of the reservation delineated by Gen. William J. Worth at the conclusion of hostilities, and a trading post was established at Charlotte Harbor.[3] Until that time only a few whites had ever penetrated the

2. Charles H. Fairbanks, "Ethnohistorical Report of the Florida Indians," passim.

3. John T. Sprague, *The Origin, Progress, and Conclusion of the Florida War*, p. 511. On November 17, 1843, Gen. William J. Worth wrote that "They plant and hunt diligently; and take their game and skins to the trading establishment or Fort Brooke, procure the necessaries they desire, and return quietly to their grounds" (pp. 507–8). However, writing in 1845 Sprague recalled that "to prevent their passing through the settlements, a trading house has been established at Charlotte's Harbor, one hundred miles south of this post, to which they can resort . . ." (p. 511). By the time that he had prepared his manuscript (pub. 1848), Sprague reported: "Occasionally a few come in to Fort Brooke to trade, but they generally confine themselves to the trading-house within the boundary" (p. 513). Nevertheless, the Seminoles did continue to make their way as far north as Tampa to trade. The sutler at Fort Brooke was Thomas P. Kennedy, who later operated the trading house at Charlotte Harbor. This trading house burned in 1848 (James W. Covington, "The Florida Seminoles in 1847," p. 51). Kennedy was the first permanent Indian trader at Tampa, and his store was located near the mouth of the Hillsborough River (Anthony P. Pizzo, *Tampa Town*, p. 23). Kennedy was active in the Third Seminole War as a supplier of ammunition and goods to the army and Florida Volunteers under the firm name of Kennedy and Darling (D. B. McKay, *Pioneer Florida*, 2:564).

heart of the Everglades—most notably the old Indian fighter, Col. William S. Harney, who tracked the Seminoles to their island camps and fought on their own terrain; and Navy Lt. John T. McLaughlin, who led the first successful crossing of the sawgrass by a military force.[4] Except for these earlier military incursions and an occasional hunting or trapping party that ventured there, the tip of the peninsula remained uninhabited by white settlers. In great part its continued isolation at a time in the nation's history when the western frontiers were being pushed toward the Pacific Ocean was due to two factors: the great difficulty of travel, and a paucity of rich, easily cultivated land for homesteads. There were also tales, often outlandishly embellished by travelers, of sweltering, insect-ridden summers, malarial swamps, and ferocious alligators or other predators awaiting the unwary. All in all, it appeared to be an unlikely place over which to fight a war with a handful of Indians; yet, this is where the last act of the Seminole wars in Florida would be played between 1855 and 1858, as the national government made a final, futile effort to dislodge the Seminoles from their homeland.

In the thirteen years of peace between the Second and Third Seminole wars, the tribal remnant that remained in Florida had adjusted to their new milieu. They settled in widely dispersed villages around the northern shore of Lake Okeechobee, up the Kissimmee River as far as Lakes Kissimmee and Tohopekaliga, on Fish Eating Creek and Lake Istopoga, as well as in the Everglades and Big Cypress proper. An estimated four hundred Seminoles—men, women, and children—were then living in southern Florida.[5] Of this number, somewhat less than a majority were Mikasukis, a Hitchiti-speaking group descended from the Lower Creeks who first came into Spanish Florida in the 1700s. The remainder were Muskogee-speaking Seminoles who were linguistically related to the Upper Creeks.[6] While these languages are closely related, they are not mutually intelligible, and that fact impeded full communication between the groups. Although by mid-century there were

4. John K. Mahon, History of the Second Seminole War, pp. 283–84, 289.
5. James W. Covington, "An Episode in the Third Seminole War," p. 48.
6. Sprague, Origin, Progress, and Conclusion, p. 507. On November 17, 1843, Gen. W. J. Worth reported that the Indians remaining in Florida were Seminoles, Mikasukis, Creeks, and Tallahassees. Captain Sprague, however, found that there were Seminole, Mikasuki, Creek, and Uchee elements among the Florida Indians (p. 510). Sprague later added Choctaws to this group prior to the publication of his book, p. 512.

some intermarriages and perhaps some common religious observances, the bands did not form a tribal entity in the accepted sense of the term; they remained functionally autonomous units which could join together in times of crisis or common need. The leader of the Muskogee-speaking elements was Chief Chipco, who kept his permanent camp well north of Lake Okeechobee.[7] Among the Indians who lived southwest of the big lake, the acknowledged leader was a hereditary Seminole chief known as Billy Bowlegs (Holata Micco).[8] Bowlegs was born to the Seminole "royal line" which lived in the vicinity of the Alachua prairie in northern Florida; he won great distinction as a leader in the Second Seminole War and was still at large heading a contingent of warriors at the conclusion of hostilities. The venerable old Mikasuki chief Sam Jones (Arpeika) was still alive, but his advanced age and growing senility precluded a leadership role in the troubles to come.

The federal Swamp Lands Act of 1850 returned all swamp lands to the states for reclamation, and suddenly the heretofore useless Everglades had great investment potential for the land development companies and railroads which had rights to vast tracts of submerged acreage. They brought great pressure to bear to survey the Southwest Florida frontier, launch drainage programs, and open the region for settlement. The Seminoles became alarmed and angered as an ever increasing number of army survey parties and white homesteaders crossed into the country between Pease Creek and the Caloosahatchee River. This influx inevitably led to clashes between the Indians and newcomers which resulted in the deaths of a number of whites; these depredations, in turn, led to a renewed agitation for total removal of all Indians from the state. Various attempts were made to persuade Billy Bowlegs and his followers to emigrate to the Indian Territory, but the wily old chief refused to be budged; he worked to maintain peaceful relations with the settlers, even to the point of turning in for punishment some of the warriors involved in the deaths of settlers.[9] Nevertheless, the pressure for removal continued to mount, and ultimately the frontier was set aflame as the Seminoles retaliated for abuses to their persons and property. Actually, the Third Seminole War was ignited by an act of flagrant

7. Covington, "An Episode," p. 48.
8. Kenneth W. Porter, "Billy Bowlegs (Holata Micco) in the Seminole Wars," passim, esp. pp. 219–42.
9. Ibid., p. 229.

vandalism perpetrated against Chief Billy Bowlegs, perhaps with the intent of provoking him into an armed response which would justify military intervention. If that was the case, the provocateurs were successful—with fatal consequences to themselves.

In December of 1855, 2d Lt. George L. Hartsuff, U.S. Army Engineers, commanded a party of eleven men running a survey line south of Fort Myers.[10] They penetrated deep into the Big Cypress country, and ten days out were camped within two miles of Billy Bowlegs' permanent camp. The troops entered the camp, which was deserted at the time, and before they left, destroyed a fine stand of banana trees growing in the chief's garden plot. When an enraged Bowlegs confronted the soldiers, he received neither compensation nor apology. The following morning the Mikasuki warriors attacked Lieutenant Hartsuff's command, killing four soldiers and wounding four others, including the lieutenant himself. When the survivors managed to make their way back to Fort Myers and spread the alarm that the Seminoles were in arms, the Third Seminole War had begun. Before the conflict ended three years later, federal and state forces numbering over fourteen hundred men had taken the field against an estimated hundred Seminole warriors. Even though outnumbered 15 to 1, the Seminoles were a formidable foe. Resorting to the hit-and-run guerrilla tactics they had used with such telling effect in the previous war, they kept the regular army and Florida mounted volunteer units off balance, so that they could never bring their superior force to bear in open pitched battle. It became a war of attrition, and in the long run the superior forces of the army and militia prevailed by destroying the Indians' source of supply, cutting off contact between the bands, and pursuing the hostiles to their Everglades hideouts as in the previous conflict. Ultimately, the Seminoles were left with little choice but surrender or extermination.

In May of 1858, Bowlegs led his band of 125 men, women, and children into Fort Myers and accepted the government indemnity of $6,500 for himself, $1,000 for each of four sub-chiefs, $500 for each warrior, and $100 for each woman and child; they then boarded the steamer *Grey Cloud* for removal to the Indian Territory west of the Mississippi River.[11] At Egmont Key a band of 40

10. Ibid., p. 236. See also Ray B. Seley, Jr., "Lieutenant Hartsuff and the Banana Plants," pp. 3–14; John C. Gifford, *Billy Bowlegs and the Seminole War*.

11. Covington, "An Episode," p. 239.

Seminoles who had been captured by Florida Volunteers was added to the party. On the day following the departure of this group, the commander in the field, Col. Gustavus Loomis, wrote the Adjutant General, U.S. Army, announcing that the third and last of the Seminole wars had come to an end: "I have the honor to report that I have this day issued a proclamation declaring the Florida war closed. Last evening Colonel Elias Rector, superintendent of Indian affairs with the delegation of friendly Indians, and the chief, Billy Bowlegs, and one hundred and sixty five hostiles—men, women, and children—left Tampa Bay on the United States steamboat 'Grey Cloud,' for New Orleans, on their way to their homes in the west."[12]

Although the army had declared the war at an end and the hostiles duly pacified, it was also aware that a number of Seminoles remained in Florida from the report of Col. Elias Rector, based upon his conversations with Billy Bowlegs on board the *Grey Cloud*: "Of those left in Florida are the parties of Sam Jones, seventeen men (twelve active warriors and five very old men), the Boat party, containing twelve men and one boy capable of bearing arms, and the Tallahassees, of whom little is known, but from the best information had is supposed to number eight warriors."[13] There was no specific enumeration of women and children in this report. Rector further noted that, in Bowlegs' opinion, the Tallahassee and Boat party, if found, would probably emigrate, as they had relatives on board the ship; however, he did not believe that Sam Jones' band would leave willingly as long as their old leader remained alive. It was suggested by Colonel Rector and the Indians that no further action be taken against the remaining groups until they had been contacted and given an opportunity to emigrate in peace. Colonel Loomis, having declared the war closed, did not consider further field operations against the stragglers, but he did request that a small delegation of Indians be left behind to contact the others. His request was not honored, and throughout the summer of 1858 the army scouts were unsuccessful in their attempts to make contact with the Seminoles; occasionally they would find camps, planted fields, and recently abandoned cookfires, but never any Indians. Thus, in the fall of that year a group of Seminoles led by Billy Bowlegs was returned to Florida, under the supervision of Colonel Rec-

12. U.S., Congress, House, *Report of the Secretary of War*, Exec. Doc. 2, 35th Cong., 2d sess., 1858, pp. 241–42.
13. Ibid., pp. 242–43.

tor, for the purpose of making contact with their kinsmen and encouraging them to relocate.[14] They did succeed in making contact but could convince only seventy-five of the remaining Seminoles to go west. The delegation returned to the Indian Territory early in 1859, and that was the last overt official attempt to effect removal of Indians from Florida.

With the coming of the Civil War, the energies of the federal military were directed elsewhere, and the Seminole bands in Florida were left in relative peace. Although there were implied threats of continued state action against the Indians, this never materialized, and their isolation in South Florida kept them out of the main action between Union and Confederate forces. It was a time of adjustment to a new life style in the lower peninsula, of recovering from the traumatic effects of almost constant turmoil for nearly two generations, and of establishing social and economic relationships between the remaining bands. Little is known of Seminole development during the early part of this period, for they had few contacts with settlers in the state. With good cause, they distrusted all whites, the vast majority of whom believed that all Indians should be removed to the Indian Territory or at least confined to some type of reservation within the state. That sentiment was apparent in a group of letters from Florida citizens submitted to the U.S. Senate Committee on Indian Affairs in March 1869. In his letter of transmittal, the Secretary of the Interior, O. H. Browning, referred to the "remnant of the tribe of Seminole Indians now living in or near the Everglades in South Florida."[15] It was probably an apt description of the Seminoles at that time—a remnant culture. In fact, they were a remnant of a remnant that was left in the state following the Second Seminole War. Cut off from the psychological support and leadership of their kinsmen in political, social, and religious matters, they had to evolve new modes of coping with existing conditions. Certainly three distinct groups, occupying different territory (though hunting widely), and even speaking different languages, would find it difficult, if not impossible, to form a unified tribal entity. Instead, what evolved over the years was a form of regionalism adapted to the peculiar needs of the Seminole people. The nature of this tri-

14. Porter, "Billy Bowlegs," p. 241. See also Edwin C. McReynolds, *The Seminoles*, p. 287; Grant Foreman, *The Five Civilized Tribes*, p. 275.
15. U.S., Congress, Senate, *Report of the Secretary of the Interior*, Exec. Doc. 35, 40th Cong., 3d sess., 1869, p. 4.

partite arrangement would occupy the attention of various researchers and observers during the last quarter of the nineteenth century, and in some cases would not be fully understood until well into this century.

Sequestered in their wilderness enclaves, the Seminoles continued to exhibit what has been described as "one of the outstanding attributes of these Indians—namely, their remarkable ability to accomplish a swift succession of successful ethnoecologic changes."[16] Through the upheaval of three wars in the period 1818–58, the Seminoles had steadily been moving away from their Creek cultural origins. As they were inexorably moved southward down the Florida peninsula by the successive application of military force and encroaching settlement, they quickly developed mechanisms to cope with their new environments. Methods of subsistence changed from large scale stock raising and communal farming endeavors by entire villages, to widely scattered small-plot cultivation by family units, with heavy dependence on hunting, fishing, and gathering of native plants. The type of settlement and nature of dwellings also changed; the substantial cabin-type structures of the northern prairie gave way to the thatched-roof, open-sided structures that were quickly constructed and better suited to the environment. These "chickees" were hidden away in small family clusters or camps rather than in large villages. Lightweight, loosely fitting clothes replaced the buckskins of the woodlands. The mode of transportation also changed as the Seminoles began to hunt and live in the watery Everglades region. Never "horse Indians," the Seminoles had typically traveled and hunted afoot; later they made full use of highly functional, shallow-draft dugout canoes made from cypress logs, and learned to navigate the trackless sawgrass or, with sail, to cross Lake Okeechobee and even put out to sea. These changes were facilitated by the adaptation of new implements and ideas gained through contacts with Negro as well as white settlers, military personnel, and traders. The last phase of this ethnoecologic adaptation took place unhampered by constant warfare and while the Indians were out of direct contact and competition with the white man.

Throughout the 1870s there was continuing agitation in Florida for the removal of the remaining Seminole bands. An investigation was ostensibly made in 1872, yet the Commissioner of Indian Af-

16. Alan K. Craig and Christopher Peebles, "Ethnoecologic Change among the Seminoles: 1740–1840."

fairs took no action and later admitted that "little has been known or heard of them since the Seminole War."[17] In 1875, Frederick A. Ober published a brief account of his contacts with the Seminoles living north of Lake Okeechobee, but it was far from a systematic study.[18] The first serious attempt to investigate post-removal Seminole culture in Florida was that of Lt. Richard Henry Pratt, founder of the Carlisle Indian Industrial School and one of the most significant figures in Indian educational history. He was selected because of prior experience in supervising a group of western tribesmen who had been incarcerated at Fort Marion in St. Augustine during 1875–78; his reward was to be the allocation of the Carlisle military barracks for the Indian school project.[19] Pratt was to ascertain how the Indians would view the possibility of removal; in addition, he was to "make a full investigation, as to their present status, and report fully, as to all the facts in the case, which will aid the office to a full understanding of their present condition . . . making in connection therewith such recommendations as you shall deem proper."[20] Unfortunately, the Florida newspapers played up that aspect of Pratt's visit relating to possible removal, and he felt that they prejudiced the outcome of his mission. Nevertheless, he agreed to undertake the assignment and submitted a report in two parts during August and September of 1879. His report provided the first official look at Seminole culture during the post–Civil War era, and it discouraged any further governmental efforts to persuade these Indians to emigrate to the Indian Territory.

Upon his arrival at Fort Meade in Polk County, Pratt found that the Seminoles were divided into four communities. Thirty miles northeast of Fort Meade was a Creek village ruled by the old chief, Chipco, whose people claimed a separate tribal origin from the others and spoke a different but related language. The second community was located on the western border of Lake Okeechobee,

17. *Annual Report of the Commissioner of Indian Affairs to the Secretary of the Interior for the Year 1875* (Department of the Interior Edition: Washington, 1875), p. 87. Quoted in William C. Sturtevant, ed., "R. H. Pratt's Report on the Seminole in 1879," p. 1.

18. Frederick A. Ober, "Ten Days with the Seminoles," pp. 142–44, 171–73.

19. Richard H. Pratt, *Battlefield and Classroom*, pp. 205–12; Jessie H. Meyer, "Development of Technical-Vocational Education at the Carlisle Indian Industrial School," pp. 1–20; Omega G. East, "Apache Indians in Fort Marion, 1886–1887," pp. 20–38. The definitive treatment of Pratt's mission to the Florida Seminoles is found in Sturtevant, "R. H. Pratt's Report," pp. 1–25.

20. Sturtevant, "R. H. Pratt's Report," p. 4.

near Fort Center, under the rule of Chief Tuscanugga. Old Chief
Tiger Tail governed a third community in the vicinity of Fort
Shackleford on the fringe of the Big Cypress Swamp, while his son,
Young Tiger Tail, had a village on the coast near present-day Miami.
Pratt attempted to bring these chiefs together to sound out their
views on removal, but he had limited success despite the intercession
of some proven white friends of the Seminoles. The prevailing view
of the Indian chiefs was that they did not want to hear any "Washington talk" or accept any aid from the federal government. This
led Pratt to the assessment that "It is probable that so long as the
old Indians remain, who passed through the war of 1835 and the
later wars of 1852–, 56 & 57 (who are justly suspicious of the United
States Govt.) no great progress can be made in the education and
civilization of these people."[21] As to the possibilities of removal to
the Indian Territory, he believed it "would do more for their ad-
vancement than any other plan, but, except by some unworthy
trick, they could not be procured to go there. I very much doubt
that they could be gathered into one community in Florida. To
reach them in their present divided state and exercise any authority
as Agent, would be an extremely difficult task, even should the Indians be willing to accept such authority."[22]

The one Seminole camp that Pratt visited and described in detail
(although his was not as complete an account as subsequent investi-
gators would provide), indicated that the Indians had established a
viable social and economic life and were reasonably prosperous. The
colorful Indian dress caught Pratt's attention: the men wore long
calico shirts ornamented with bright ribbon, and turbans made of
small bright shawls, and they usually went barefooted; however,
buckskin leggins, moccasins, and light hunting coats were available.
The women were attired in short jackets, skirts of calico, and great
amounts of multi-colored beads. He also noted the thatched-roof,
climate-adapted dwellings, the cultivated fields of corn, sweet potatoes, rice, and sugarcane, and the abundance of livestock, especially hogs. The presence of a well-constructed sugarcane mill was
of especial interest as evidence of technological progress; however,
the Indians displayed only a few old firearms, so Pratt inferred that
they depended primarily upon the bow and arrow for hunting. The
aura of overall prosperity in the camp led Pratt to estimate a cash

21. Ibid., p. 14.
22. Ibid.

income of $6,000 annually from the sale of pelts, livestock, and pro-
duce—probably an inflated figure for that period. The Seminoles in
this region were still trading in Tampa, Fort Meade, and Bartow,
and the period of volume buying in plumes and hides had not yet
begun. Nevertheless, he described a self-sufficient, independent
people who neither wanted nor needed outside help.

It was difficult to ascertain the exact number of Seminoles inhab-
iting the camp since all attempts to obtain such information were
rebuffed by the Indians. With the aid of his interpreter and guide,
Pratt learned that twenty-six persons, six of whom were warriors,
lived in Chipco's camp. In addition, there were three Negroes reportedly held as property, and Pratt added almost as an after-
thought that "as late as last year, Chipco offered to sell negroes, at
$800.00 each, in Fort Meade."[23] After consulting with prominent
white settlers such as Capt. F. A. Hendry, who had helped him contact the other Seminole camps in South Florida, Pratt estimated the
total Indian population at 292, although he believed that to be
higher than the actual number.

During his brief visit, Pratt, who was not a trained ethnographer,
made no attempt to learn the clan relationships existing among the
Seminoles. Neither did he delve into the political structure or religious practices of the people. On certain points he was inclined
to judge the Indians by a somewhat puritanical standard of behav-
ior. His overweening concern with the accessibility of liquor at the
trading posts led him, for example, to make the pejorative statement that "their annual green corn dance, held when roasting ears
come, usually turns out a great drunken frolic."[24] Undeniably, the
Indians bought liquor from the town saloonkeepers and often drank
to excess; however, Pratt apparently was unaware of the religious
significance of the green corn dance and the use of the "black drink"
in the religious purification rites. It is highly unlikely that gross in-
toxication would have been tolerated by the medicine man on such
an occasion, though drinking well might have occurred near the time
of the corn dance proper. Although many aspects of the culture were
overlooked, the information which Pratt compiled enabled him to
draw a number of conclusions about the Seminoles and to make
certain recommendations concerning their education, as requested
by the Commissioner of Indian Affairs. Primarily, he recommended

23. Ibid., p. 8.
24. Ibid., p. 12.

sending a teacher to the camps to instruct the children, help with agricultural and livestock problems, and generally build good will. The second step would be to establish an industrial training school for Indians in Florida, possibly at old Fort Brooke in Tampa, where the youths could be sent to further their formal education and also learn a useful trade. This was essentially the plan that Pratt had devised for the Carlisle School, and he considered it a paradigm for all Indian education in the United States.

Pratt's report was not printed until 1888, and perhaps because of this delay, there were no further governmental efforts to contact and educate the Seminoles for over a decade. However, informal efforts to facilitate Indian schooling did not cease. In August 1879, Capt. F. A. Hendry of Fort Myers, whom Pratt described as "one of the largest cattle owners in the state, a worthy and warm friend of the Indians, and one of the few in whom they confide,"[25] wrote to announce a major breakthrough in getting a Seminole into school. Billy Conapatchee, a young Seminole whom the townspeople called by a combination of his anglicized and Indian names, lived with the Hendry family for three years and attended the Fort Myers Academy. There are no extant records of his work, but Hendry and others reported that he made good progress in learning to read and write English.[26] When the Reverend Clay MacCauley conducted a survey of the Seminoles for the Smithsonian Institution in 1880–81, Billy Conapatchee served as his guide and interpreter. In his report MacCauley noted that the boy had been studying the white man's language and ways for more than a year, and "at that time he was the only Seminole who had separated himself from his people and had cast his lot with the whites."[27] Billy's decision to learn the white man's ways brought him into grave conflict with his people; the tribal elders condemned him, and only the pleas of his father saved his life. Even so, there was at least one overt threat against the young Indian's life by another Seminole over this matter, and Captain Hendry had to intervene in the affair. MacCauley was greatly impressed by the alertness and perseverance of his guide, and based largely on this contact wrote that "if the Seminole are to be judged by comparison with other American aborigines, I believe

25. Ibid., p. 6.
26. Ibid., p. 17. Also see *Fort Myers Press*, March 7, 1885, p. 2; Clay MacCauley, "The Seminole Indians of Florida," pp. 492–94; *Miami Herald*, Feb. 5, 1967, p. 14A.
27. MacCauley, "The Seminole Indians of Florida," p. 492.

they easily enter the first class."[28] Billy Conapatchee's success in learning to read and write was taken by Pratt as a signal that the Seminole people were ready to accept education, and he made plans to get some of them into the Carlisle School.[29] However, Billy was an isolated case. By 1885 he had returned to his home in the Everglades, and no other Seminole—not even his children—came seeking the white man's school. Evidently the tribal elders had firmly discouraged further movement in this direction.

MacCauley's survey of the Seminole Indians in Florida was a more extensive and complete account than that rendered by Pratt a year earlier. During his three month sojourn in South Florida through the winter of 1880–81, he was able to visit every known camp, and he compiled an impressive amount of data, including the first modern census of the Indian population in the state. He located 208 Indians living in five major villages: the four identified by Pratt, plus one on a small stream northeast of Lake Okeechobee which he identified as the Cow Creek settlement. If his identification of the two northern camps as being "Tallahassee Indians" who considered themselves different from the three lower camps was correct (Pratt called one of these camps "Creeks" and did not locate the other), then the division of the Indian population at that time would logically have been 40 Creek and 168 Mikasuki speakers; however, this figure is disputable.[30] It is possible that the Cow Creek settlement did not exist at the time of Pratt's visit, or it might have been the place where a group of Chipco's people had moved.

There were a number of points on which MacCauley and Pratt differed drastically, and in most cases the former's report must be given more consideration due to his length of stay, preciseness of observation, and prior experience with native cultures. For example, MacCauley differentiated thirty-seven families living in twenty-

28. Ibid., p. 493.
29. Pratt, Battlefield and Classroom, p. 256.
30. MacCauley, "The Seminole Indians of Florida," pp. 508-9. The language spoken in each of the five settlements was never fully identified by MacCauley, but the clear implication was that the two northern villages at Cat Fish Lake and Cow Creek were both politically and linguistically different from the other three. However, Sturtevant ("R. H. Pratt's Report," p. 20) includes the Fish Eating Creek settlement among the Muskogee-speaking element, and thereby concludes that "MacCauley's figures give the Creek Seminole 35 percent, and in 1952 they amounted to about 36 percent of the total Seminole population." But the head chief at the Fish Eating Creek settlement, Tustanugge, was a Mikasuki-speaking Seminole (Ober, "Ten Days," p. 172).

two camps, which were gathered into five widely dispersed groups:
Pratt identified only the four villages that he knew of and their
leaders. In Chipco's village Pratt noted only the old Kentucky rifle
and bows and arrows as weapons, but alluded to the possibility of
modern weapons in the other villages; MacCauley made "a careful
count of their firearms, and found that they own 'Kentucky' rifles,
63; breech loading rifles, 8; shotgun and rifle, 1; revolvers, 2—total,
74."[31] The dependence on the old Kentucky rifle he attributed to the
Indians' remoteness from traders from whom they could obtain prepared ammunition for more modern weapons, and he thoroughly discounted the use of bow and arrow for hunting purposes. The two
observers also differed over whether the Negroes living in the Indian
camps were held in some type of servitude. MacCauley could find
no justification for such a claim, believing that they were accepted
members of the group.

One of the more significant points in MacCauley's study was his
observation on the political structure of the Seminoles. He found
them in a rather disorganized condition, but noted "there is, however, among these Indians a simple form of government, to which
the inhabitants of at least the three southern settlements submit. The
people of Cat Fish Lake and Cow Creek settlements live in a large
measure independent of or without civil connection with the
others."[32] If there was anything approximating a seat of government,
he held, it was the village on Fish Eating Creek where the annual
council for the lower villages was held under Chief Tustenugge and
the medicine men.[33] There was no identifiable political structure in
the two Creek-speaking villages north of Lake Okeechobee, although apparently a certain amount of contact existed between
them and the villages south of the lake: MacCauley found that in
the case of the Green Corn Dance, "the 'Tallahassee Indians' go to
Fish Eating Creek if they desire to take part in the festival."[34] Thus,
as early as 1880 there was a well-established tradition of group
autonomy between the Hitchiti and Muskogee elements of the Seminoles in Florida.

If the Florida Indians were divided politically and linguistically,
there were also many cultural elements that united them. Perhaps

31. MacCauley, "The Seminole Indians of Florida," p. 512.
32. Ibid., p. 508.
33. Ibid., pp. 508–9.
34. Ibid., p. 508.

most basic was their religious belief in a "Great Spirit" who ruled over the earth and protected the Indians. From the little that he could learn from his interpreter, MacCauley concluded that "the one institution at present in which the religious beliefs of the Seminole find special expression is what is called the 'Green Corn Dance.' It is the occasion for an annual purification and rejoicing. I could get no satisfactory description of the festival."[35] Nevertheless, he did piece together a few details which led him to believe that the ceremony was still very similar to the Creek busk ritual of the preceding century, a full description of which has been reported by Swanton.[36] As a minister and former missionary, MacCauley concluded that many Seminole beliefs were an amalgam of traditional and Christian ideas, perhaps due to the influence of early Spanish missionaries in Florida, but this interpretation is open to question. The Spanish mission chain was destroyed well before the Seminole ascendancy in Florida.[37]

A second cultural link between the Seminole groups which Mac-Cauley reported was that of a clan or gens system. The best translation which he could get of clan in the Seminole tongue was "those of one camp or house."[38] According to his informants, 198 of the Indians were members of nine clans: wind, tiger, otter, bird, deer, snake, bear, wolf, and alligator. No clan identity was available for ten of the Indians. The clan was described as a group of individuals tracing a common lineage to some remote ancestor. Among the Seminoles this lineage passes through the women, and all children are members of the mother's clan. There was a prohibition against individuals marrying within their own clan, as well as certain rights and obligations of membership. MacCauley did not spell out these relationships in detail, but he noted that they were the basis for

35. Ibid., p. 522. The Green Corn Dance was the primary religious ceremony of the Creek Nation, celebrated at the ripening of the new crop in late May or June. At the direction of the medicine men, the clans gathered at the prepared dancing ground. On the first day, the dancing began and the warriors took the "Black Drink," an emetic and cathartic to purify the body. The next day, the green corn could be eaten as part of the feasting. On subsequent days, the elders sat in judgment of those who had broken tribal law, adolescents were given their adult names, and major tribal business was conducted.

36. John R. Swanton, "Social Organization and Social Usages of the Indians of the Creek Confederacy," pp. 551-64.

37. Mark F. Boyd, Hale G. Smith, and John W. Griffin, Here They Once Stood, pp. 1–20.

38. MacCauley, "The Seminole Indians of Florida," p. 507.

most social and governmental organization among the Indians. It is interesting that the same comparative ranking of clans was not given in the northern and southern camps, although clan membership apparently cut across village boundaries. Assuming that tiger/puma/panther are synonymous usages, it remains the largest clan among the contemporary Seminole and Mikasuki people. There is a Seminole folk tale, perhaps apocryphal, which has it that early in this century there was but one remaining female panther clan member, a woman of the Big Cypress region; she married and had eleven children, ten of whom were girls, thus regenerating the panther clan.

In this century, a study of the Cow Creek Seminoles made by Spoehr revealed that the panther clan had retained its place of prominence to the extent that the head medicine man of the band always belonged to that clan.[39] Spoehr's work confirmed most of MacCauley's assumptions about the interworkings of the clanship system and greatly amplified the topic. Essentially, it was found that the clan, as a basic unit in Seminole life, had three major functions: first, it provided a sense of belonging to a specific group within the tribe whose members were bound to honor and support each other; second, it provided a political division to which the member could look for protection in times of stress; third, it had an important place in the ceremonial organization of the band, with each clan providing specific ceremonial offices such as medicine men, watchers who exhorted people to dance, and herb gatherers. Furthermore, among the Seminoles the clan system cross-cut the band political organization and helped unify the people.

In addition to religion and clan membership, there were many common elements of physical culture which all Seminole groups shared. It was noted that "dwellings throughout the Seminole district are practically uniform in construction," with most houses being "approximately 16 by 9 feet in ground measurement, made almost altogether, if not wholly, of materials taken from the palmetto tree. It is actually but a platform elevated about three feet from the ground and covered with palmetto thatched roof. . . . This platform is peculiar, in that it fills the interior of the building like a floor and serves to furnish the family with a dry sitting or lying down place when, as often happens, the whole region is under water. . . . The covering is, I was informed, water tight and durable

39. Alexander Spoehr, "Camp, Clan and Kin among the Cow Creek Seminoles of Florida," pp. 14–16.

and will resist even a violent wind. Only hurricanes can tear it off, and these are so infrequent in Southern Florida that no attempt is made to provide against them."[40]

MacCauley was particularly impressed with the physical characteristics, dress, and ornamentation of the Seminole people. The men he found admirable for their muscular power and endurance, and their costume of knee-length shirt, breech cloth, neckerchiefs, turban, and pouch belt was a model of efficiency for the active life they led in that humid, semitropical climate. For example, the Seminole turban, made of a small folded shawl, was used to carry personal items such as pipe and tobacco which could not fit into the pouches containing bullets, flint, and powder; the neckerchiefs were tied in such a way that they would hold money and other small loose items, since the Indian shirt had no pockets. The shirt was cool, comfortable, and allowed freedom of movement when hunting in high water areas. The leather leggins, so common when the Seminoles lived farther north, had been relegated to mostly ceremonial functions by the time of MacCauley's study.[41]

The women MacCauley described as having dark good looks and a simple costume. Most of them wore a two-piece outfit: a short shirt with long sleeves, cut low at the neck, which barely covered the breasts, and a long skirt of dark colored calico or gingham which extended to the ground. The women's skirts were relatively devoid of decoration, with just a little trim around the bottom, perhaps due to the lack of sewing machines.[42] However, what they lacked in clothing decoration they made up for with quantities of beads worn about the neck while working in camp or field, or visiting other settlements.[43] Occasionally, both men and women wore silver disks fashioned from coins, and some rings, but gold ornaments were never seen. At this time the Seminole men were still wearing their traditional hair style of hair cropped close except for bangs across the front, and a strip from the crown to nape of the neck terminating in queues. The women gathered their hair into elongated cones at the neck, often tied with ribbon, and wore bangs over the forehead. To the extent that information was available,

40. MacCauley, "The Seminole Indians of Florida," p. 500.
41. Ibid., p. 484.
42. John M. Goggin, "Florida's Indians," p. 3. Goggin wrote that "in 1880 there was a single sewing machine in the tribe."
43. MacCauley, "The Seminole Indians of Florida," pp. 487–88.

MacCauley gave equally detailed descriptions of hunting, fishing, agriculture, mortuary practices, marriage rites, child rearing, and everyday life about the Indian camps.

In summarizing his impressions of the Seminoles, MacCauley expressed admiration for the way in which they had adapted to the environment and developed strength in isolation from the dominant white culture. But he cautioned that "man is becoming a factor of new importance in their environment. The moving lines of the white population are closing in upon the land of the Seminole. There is no further retreat to which they can go."[44] He hoped that a stable relationship could be developed between the Indians and the settlers, but prophesied that "soon a great and rapid change must take place . . . the Seminole is about to enter a future unlike any past he has known."[45] This prediction of rapid cultural change was truer than even MacCauley imagined at the time. The attempts to drain the Everglades and develop large-scale agriculture, the surveying and distribution of lands for homesteading, and the increasing interest in South Florida as a source for plumes and other trade goods, would bring a flood of whites into the region before the turn of the century. Thus, the studies by Pratt and MacCauley reveal a Seminole culture as it had developed in relative isolation during the two decades that had elapsed since the Third Seminole War, and they must stand as benchmarks for ethnographers and historians who would chronicle the immense changes in Indian life over the next century.

By the 1880s Florida was in the midst of its first "land boom" as a result of Hamilton Disston's drainage and development program in the Kissimmee River–Lake Okeechobee–Caloosahatchee River region.[46] Also, great national interest in Florida had been generated by the New Orleans *Times-Democrat* expeditions of 1882 and 1883 which crossed the Everglades.[47] A tide of settlers came seeking cheap land, and it was not long before the pressure which MacCauley had

44. Ibid., p. 530.
45. Ibid., p. 531.
46. Pat Dodson, "Hamilton Disston's St. Cloud Sugar Plantation, 1887–1901," pp. 356–69. Junius E. Dovell, "The Railroads and the Public Lands of Florida, 1879–1905," pp. 238–40.
47. Morgan Dewey Peoples and Edwin Adams Davis, eds., "Across South Central Florida in 1882: the Account of the First New Orleans *Times-Democrat* Exploring Expedition," pp. 49–88, 63–92; Wintringham, "North to South through the Glades in 1883," pp. 33–93.

predicted began to mount against the Seminoles. Most of the lands upon which they had settled were owned by individuals, railroads, or land development companies anxious to be rid of the Indians. Repeated complaints from both foes and friends of the Seminoles led to congressional action to alleviate the situation. A provision of the Indian appropriation act of July 1884, allocated a sum of $6,000 "to enable the Seminole Indians in Florida to obtain homesteads upon the public lands and to establish themselves thereon."[48] A special government agent, Cyrus Beede, was appointed and spent several months during the winter of 1884–85 trying to carry out the provisions of the act, but with no success. He did succeed in convincing some Indians to take homesteads but could find no vacant federal land upon which to settle them, so the funds reverted to the Treasury.

Friction between the Seminoles and white settlers continued, and in January 1887, A. M. Wilson was appointed Special Agent to attempt again to carry out the congressional intention of settling the Florida Indians on land of their own. His two reports to the Commissioner of Indian Affairs were anything but encouraging about the prospect of resettling the Seminoles on land not of their choosing. During his visits to the Indian camps in Polk, Brevard, Monroe, and Dade counties, Wilson took an informal census and estimated the population at 269; of these, 60 were males twenty-one years of age or older.[49] Perhaps still anticipating trouble, he estimated that with the addition of young men who were accomplished hunters, the Indians could muster 200 fighting men—an extraordinary claim considering that the recently conducted MacCauley report showed only 112 males of all ages.

Special Agent Wilson's report was accepted by the Commissioner of Indian Affairs and transmitted to the Senate Committee on Indian Affairs. In his letter of transmittal, the commissioner recommended that the remaining monies be used to buy some homesteads for Indians and included the draft of a bill authorizing this use, which he urged Congress to accept. There was an undeniable note of urgency in the commissioner's plea that "increasing white settle-

48. U.S., Congress, Senate, *Message from the President of the United States Transmitting a Letter of the Secretary of the Interior Relative to Land upon Which to Locate Seminole Indians*, Exec. Doc. 139, 50th Cong., 1st sess., 1888, p. 2.
49. Ibid., p. 7.

ments in southern Florida are fast driving these people from their accustomed haunts and depriving them of their means of support. It is charged that they kill cattle belonging to the large herds in that section of the state, to the value of some $2,000 to $3,000 annually. In view of these facts, trouble between them and the whites is likely to occur at any time."[50] Nevertheless, the Indian appropriation act of 1888 earmarked $6,000 "for support and education of the Seminole and Creek Indians in Florida, for the erection and furnishing of a schoolhouse, for the employment of teachers, and for purchase of seeds and agricultural implements and other necessary articles,"[51] but made no provision for the purchase of lands.

At this point a new champion of the Seminoles appeared in the person of Miss Lilly Pierpont of Winter Haven. She had become alarmed at the plight of the Indians living near her home and decided to make a direct appeal, woman to woman, to the wife of the President. In January 1887 she wrote to Mrs. Grover Cleveland, detailing the injustice done the Seminoles, and implored her to take the issue to her husband:

> If I write, Mrs. Cleveland, to Florida's Representatives they will pay no attention to my letter. The average man never exerts himself, except for himself, until forced to it, and I have not the strength to give the required pressure. The men here to whom I have mentioned the subject say, "The Indians will soon be exterminated;" "The white man will shortly put an end to the last of them;" "They are happier as they are;" "The Indians are an ungrateful people;" "They have not the minds for receiving education," etc. How can they be grateful for benefits never received? How can we form an idea of their mental capacity before it is tested?
>
> I can not forget that this great country was once all theirs. Nor do I think it will cost the Government more to give the Seminoles a few acres of land in a healthy locality, with legal title to the same, and to provide them with a few of the many blessings we enjoy now, than in a few years to support them in forts.
>
> Will you, Mrs. Cleveland, mention this subject to Mr. Cleveland? . . .[52]

50. Ibid., p. 3.
51. U.S., Congress, House, *Report of the Commissioner of Indian Affairs*, Exec. Doc. 1, 50th Cong., 2d sess., 1888, p. 75.
52. Exec. Doc. 139, 50th Cong., 1st sess., 1888, p. 5.

The Pierpont letter was included in the Report of the Commissioner of Indian Affairs to the U.S. Senate in 1888. As a result of her obvious interest and compassion, she, too, was appointed Special Agent to see if lands could be found upon which to settle the Seminole people. After a year of frustration, Miss Pierpont resigned the commission, and her successor also met with failure. The Seminoles were once more left without official representation in the face of continued incursions into their territory.

By the end of the decade, there had been a forced migration of some Indian elements out of their traditional lands. The Creek-speaking bands had all but abandoned their camps in the upper Kissimmee River basin and were scattered around the northern rim of Lake Okeechobee, along Cow Creek, as well as in the Bluefield, Hungryland areas near Fort Pierce. The camps along Fish Eating Creek had also been abandoned in the face of large-scale cattle interests which had come into the vicinity. In the late 1880s, a small contingent of Mikasukis had moved their camps to the lower end of the Big Cypress Swamp. Along the lower east coast the influx of settlers was not as steady before the coming of the railroad in the 1890s, but already the Seminoles were beginning to abandon camps on the coastal ridge for those on hammocks in the Everglades beyond the falls of the Miami River, although they remained along the New River well into the nineties. Thus, the tripartite division of the Seminole people into Cow Creek, Miami or East Coast, and Big Cypress bands had been accomplished by the turn of the century; they would retain these positions well into the twentieth century, when each segment would form the population base for the federal reservations established during the 1920s and 1930s.

The decade of the 1890s would bring not only increased cultural contacts between the Seminoles and white society but also the first substantive attempts to improve the social and economic conditions of the Indian people in Florida. These efforts came about through the combined efforts of the federal government, religious groups, and private philanthropists who banded together to form voluntary associations to provide funds to purchase land, provide legal assistance, and generally promote the welfare of the Seminoles through lobbying activities of all types. The first organized attempt to reach and serve the Seminoles, however, came from a national organization: the Women's National Indian Association. This was one of many such groups formed in response to an awakened national consciousness of the "Indian problem" in the United States. A number of journalistic exposés such as Indian Commissioner G. W. Manypenny's *Our Indian Wards* (1879), as well as Helen Hunt Jackson's *A Century of Dishonor* (1881), and *Ramona* (1884), had touched the hearts of millions and brought outcries to redress some of the injustices done to the native peoples. The outstanding federal effort in response to this movement was the Dawes Act of 1887, which proposed to turn Indian families into freeholders of individual farm allotments rather than having tribal lands held in common as provided for by treaty; this action was brought about by the Dawes Commission of 1893. Although the Dawes Act was hailed at the time as a step in the direction of assimilating the Indian into the social and economic life of the nation, its great cost in terms of loss of personal and tribal identity, as well as the siphoning off of millions of acres of Indian lands through chicanery, is today recognized as a national tragedy for the Indian peoples.[53] Nevertheless, the American altruistic spirit had responded to this new cause célèbre in typical fashion: associations were formed to assist the Indian.

In March 1891, Mrs. Amelia S. Quinton, president of the Missionary Committee of the Women's National Indian Association, accompanied by two other ladies and Capt. F. A. Hendry, visited the Indian camps on the western edge of the Everglades. As a result of this visit the WNIA resolved to establish a mission to provide education and industrial training, as well as general missionary activities, for the Seminoles; by June the organization had purchased 400 acres for that purpose. The acreage was located forty-five miles southeast of Fort Myers and three miles east of Lake Trafford in present-day Collier County. The site selected was reportedly "comparatively high ground and not subject to overflow, except in extreme freshets" and therefore suitable for crops and permanent buildings.[54] Late that summer, Dr. and Mrs. J. E. Brecht, a missionary couple from St. Louis, arrived to begin a nine-year tenure among the Seminole people.

Shortly after the missionaries arrived, the U.S. Government purchased eighty acres of WNIA land to establish an Indian Agency,

53. Sar A. Levitan and Barbara Hetrick, *Big Brother's Indian Programs—with Reservations*, pp. 14–19.
54. U.S., Congress, House, *Report of the Commissioner of Indian Affairs*, Exec. Doc. 1, 53d Cong., 2d sess., 1893, p. 356.

and Dr. Brecht was soon appointed Disbursing Agent and Industrial Teacher.[55] Although an excellent facility was developed which included a sawmill, store, schoolhouse, and farm, the Indians never showed any inclination to take advantage of the opportunity to learn the skills of the white man. An elementary school was opened at the station, with Lee County paying half the teacher's salary for the white children in attendance and the WNIA contributing the other half for the Indian children. However, an inspector found that since no Indian children ever attended, the teacher was assigning Seminole names to the white children and reporting them to the WNIA for payment.[56] Needless to say, the school project then collapsed. Although the Indians refused to take part in the activities at the government station, they did visit often and became quite friendly with the Brechts, who were often invited to the Green Corn Dance.[57] In addition to establishing rapport with the Seminole people by visiting in their camps regularly—which he thought was the most important phase of his work—Brecht worked diligently to secure lands for the Indians and attempted to prosecute the whiskey sellers who frequented the Everglades. While he did little to reduce the flow of liquor into the Indian camps, he was quite successful in locating and purchasing lands to be held for the Seminole people. The ten thousand acres of land that he had purchased by 1897, much of it in present-day Hendry County, formed the nucleus of federal acquisitions that would eventually be turned into permanent reservations for the Seminoles during this century.[58] The Brechts left the Indian work in 1899, and there would not be another agent in the field until L. A. Spencer assumed the post in 1913. In the interim, much of the direct contact with the Seminoles living deep in the Big Cypress would be carried on by missionaries of the Protestant Episcopal Church.

In 1893, the Women's National Indian Association, finding that they could not replace Dr. Brecht with a suitable person to carry on the mission work, deeded their project to the Episcopal Missionary Jurisdiction of Southern Florida. The dynamic Bishop William Crane Gray made the Indian mission one of his special projects, and

55. U.S. Congress, House, *Report of the Commissioner of Indian Affairs,* Exec. Doc. 5, 55th Cong., 2d sess., 1897, p. 125.

56. Charlton W. Tebeau, *Florida's Last Frontier,* p. 71.

57. Charles H. Coe, *Red Patriots: The Story of the Seminoles,* p. 247.

58. Roy Nash, "Survey of the Seminole Indians of Florida," Senate Doc. 314, 71st Cong., 1st sess., February 28, 1931, pp. 62–63.

on his first visit he named the site Immokalee, which means "my home" in the Mikasuki language spoken by the Indians of the region.[59] By 1895 a missionary couple, the Reverend and Mrs. H. O. Gibbs, had been installed at the Immokalee mission; a new church was added the following year, and Bishop Gray held the first services with "some Indians" in attendance.[60] The Bishop was also interested in reaching the Seminoles on their hunting grounds, just as the traders were doing, particularly after the Immokalee community began to grow and the Indians came in less frequently. He thus decided to buy a tract of land within three miles of where W. H. "Bill" Brown had established his first Indian trading post. In 1898 the Glade Cross mission was established as an outpost where the missionaries could spend several months each year. A medical missionary, Dr. W. J. Godden, established a hospital for Indians at the Glade Cross mission shortly after his arrival there in 1905; when "Bill" Brown decided to sell his trading post in 1908, Bishop Gray purchased the "Boat Landing" and moved the Episcopal mission there. Dr. Godden continued to run the store there as well as the hospital until the mission was moved again in 1913, this time to higher land near Fort Shackleford, where an industrial training farm was established. When Dr. Godden died in 1914, the mission closed and was never reopened by the church.

While the Mikasuki elements south of Lake Okeechobee had received the bulk of federal and private efforts during the 1890s, the smaller Cow Creek band living north of the lake was not without its champions. Perhaps the best known of these were Mr. and Mrs. J. M. Willson of Kissimmee, who led the fight for Indian lands until the establishment of a state reservation in 1917. In 1896, Minnie Moore-Willson published *The Seminoles of Florida*, which was the first book on the Florida Indians since the Seminole Wars. It was followed in 1898 by Charles H. Coe's *Red Patriots: The Story of the Seminoles*. The Willsons, along with Bishop William C. Gray, the writer Kirk Munroe, F. A. Hendry, and a number of other prominent

59. "Bishop's Journal," *Journal of the Eighth Annual Convocation of the Church in the Missionary Jurisdiction of Southern Florida* (Tampa, 1900), p. 60. Confirmed in an interview with Rose Brown Kennon, Fort Myers, September 24, 1971. Tape and transcript in University of Florida Indian Oral History Archives, Florida State Museum, Gainesville.

60. "Bishop's Journal," *Journal of the Fifth Annual Convocation of the Church in the Missionary Jurisdiction of Southern Florida* (Tampa, 1897), p. 71.

business and civic leaders, formed the "Friends of the Florida Seminoles" organization which purchased lands, provided legal defense, lobbied in the legislature, and generally promoted the cause of the Seminoles at the turn of the century. The Willson home in Kissimmee was a focal point for this activity, and well known Indians such as the old chief Tallahassee, Tom Tiger, Billy Bowlegs III, and many others, often visited there. On the lower west coast at Fort Myers, families like that of Dr. William Hanson and his son W. Stanley, as well as the Hendrys, offered a haven for Indians who had made the trek in from the Big Cypress to conduct their business in town, and such visits became more frequent. Thus, by the turn of the century, the Seminoles were slowly beginning to expand their social contacts with the non-Indian majority in Florida, at first visiting with known friends, then gradually expanding their economic and recreational activities in those communities where they were accepted. In many towns they were considered quaint cultural anachronisms, in others they were ostracized, while in many they were a natural element of community life—and the Seminoles almost instinctively knew the status that they were accorded by the townspeople.

In this process of gradual acculturation, the Indians continued to turn to those trading families they had known and trusted for many years. Often the old trading posts had metamorphosed into local "general stores" with the growth of settlements, while less and less of their business was based on the Indian trade; yet these stores remained the focal point for the Indians who had been coming there for years. As long as they remained in operation, the Girtman Grocery in Miami, Stranahan's Mercantile Co. in Fort Lauderdale, as well as the Meserve and Raulerson stores in Okeechobee, remained favorite haunts of the Seminoles; some are still doing business to this day with the grandsons and granddaughters of the Indians who brought in pelts, plumes, and hides during the 1890s. In the following pages we shall explore those reciprocal relationships—both social and economic—which developed between the Seminoles and trading families during the last quarter of the nineteenth century and the first three decades of the present century. The focus is on those permanent trading posts which were established to serve a frontier population but made their greatest profit from the Indian trade. The accounts of life at these outposts are colorful narratives of cultural interaction, and if there is a thread of similarity in the experiences, there is also diversity in terms of the differing needs, strong personalities, and interpersonal stresses that existed. And, perhaps most importantly, there is the story of how the whites and the Seminoles learned to live together, often forging bonds of friendship that have lasted to this day.

2

The Miami Traders

Brickell to Burdine

WILLIAM Barnwell Brickell was not the first white trader to settle
along the shores of Biscayne Bay in the latter half of the nineteenth
century, but he was by far the best known and most successful of
those who exploited the Seminole trade in that region. As early as
1844 Robert Fletcher had acquired ten acres of land on the south
side of the Miami River and presumably established a store. He remained there until 1870; later Charles Barnes bought the holding
and continued trading with the Indians until he died of yellow
fever.[1] Another well known trader was "French Mike" Sayers, who
was reportedly selling whiskey to Indians from a "dirty shanty" in
1866.[2] During this same period there was also another trader sup-
posedly doing business near the rapids on the river. Other than
Brickell, however, none of these left a lasting impression on the small
community that was to become Miami.

In 1870, Brickell and his friend E. T. Sturtevant of Cleveland,
Ohio, first arrived at Biscayne Bay. Both were successful businessmen seeking a freer way of life than they had known in the North,

1. "Abstract of Title, Mrs. Hagan (or Rebecca Egan) Donation, January 16,
1907." Robbins, Graham & Chillingworth, Examining Counsel, Miami, Florida.
Copy in possession of the author, courtesy of the Historical Association of
Southern Florida. This document verifies that Fletcher and Barnes held title
to a ten-acre tract on the south side of the Miami River. The trading activities
are set out in "Reminiscenses of Mrs. A. C. Richards, 1903," a collection of
papers in the possession of Mrs. Arva Parks, Coral Gables, Florida. For an
account of Barnes' death due to yellow fever, see Ralph Middleton Munroe
and Vincent Gilpin, *The Commodore's Story*, pp. 94–95.
2. George R. Bentley, "Colonel Thompson's Tour of Tropical Florida," p. 9.

and having found the tropical Eden they sought, each decided to remain permanently. The two friends soon had a dispute over land titles, and Sturtevant resettled farther north on the bay. The family moved back to Ohio following Sturtevant's death, but his married daughter, Julia Tuttle, later returned to the Miami area and acquired a section of land on the north side of the river which included old Fort Dallas, where she made her home. Mrs. Tuttle would ultimately use these land holdings to entice Henry M. Flagler into extending his Florida East Coast Railroad to Miami.

The Brickells purchased land on the south side of the Miami River and along the New River farther north in Dade County. By 1871 they had built a two-story wooden home and trading post on a bluff overlooking both the river and bay.[3] A second trading post, a two-story building with dock extending into the river, was completed in the early 1880s. A visitor to the area circa 1882 reported that the Brickell family lived ". . . much the same as they had five years before, but now doing a large trade with the Indians since Mr. Ewan had closed his store. The Brickells were erecting a large building on the point close to the river to take care of the increased business."[4] The palm- and shrubbery-covered site of the trading post, perhaps one of the most picturesque in South Florida at the time, still bears the name Brickell Point.

The history of the Brickell family prior to its arrival in Florida has become so embellished over the years that it borders on myth, and it is doubtful that the true story will ever emerge. The most popular and persistent version holds that the family had wealth derived from a romantic and adventurous past.[5] William Brickell was a native of Ohio who migrated to California during the 1840s and acquired a fortune. Some years later his wanderlust took him to the Orient and later Australia, where he met and married Mary Bulmer

3. Munroe and Gilpin, *The Commodore's Story*, p. 79. "Abstract of Title, 1907," attests that the Brickells acquired the 610-acre Rebecca Hagan Donation in 1870, and began living on the land on December 9, 1871. The house and store were built the same year, and a large warehouse was added in 1889. In 1871, E. T. Sturtevant filed a $2,970.42 lien claim against the property for material and labor, and this no doubt precipitated his quarrel with Brickell.

4. Charles W. Pierce, *Pioneer Life in Southeast Florida*, ed. Donald W. Curl, p. 154. Pierce originally visited the Miami River ca. 1879.

5. A highly romanticized version of the Brickell legend appears in Helen Muir, *Miami, U.S.A.* However, the same general theme is repeated in Munroe and Gilpin, *The Commodore's Story*, and countless articles and newspaper clippings.

of Yorkshire, England. Brickell apparently enjoyed perpetuating the image of a world traveler and often regaled visitors with stories of his adventures in such exotic places as "China, Australia, and New York City."[6] Of course there were also those living around Miami who debunked the Brickell stories, such as Commodore Ralph Munroe, who held that the old trader ". . . had a picturesque history, which lost no color in the telling. Some of his yarns were extraordinary, and at times doubted by many. He had strange experiences, and his vivid and colorful imagination, a natural part of the temperament which enjoyed such a life, could not resist dramatic exaggeration."[7]

Upon returning to the United States, the Brickells ostensibly moved in leading social and political circles at the time of the Civil War and later established a lucrative wholesale grocery business in Cleveland; but this has never been verified. If true, the move to a remote village on the Florida peninsula would have made it all but impossible for Brickell to continue his business; thus the trading post was essential to the family's economic survival in the years before the railroad came and the value of their land holdings soared. On the other hand, it is possible that Brickell was just another adventurer seeking his fortune on the Florida frontier by securing cheap land and operating a store for settlers and Indians alike. In either case, this strangely reclusive and eccentric family dominated the trade at Miami for a quarter of a century.

Alice, the oldest of the seven Brickell children, was in charge of the everyday operation of the store, where she created her own legend for total high-handedness in dealing with patrons. In February 1880, she was appointed postmistress of "Miami," as the station was then called, and the post office was located in the Brickell store.[8] There are stories that she showed a notable lack of concern for getting the mail distributed, often leaving letters and parcels on the table where the mail carrier had dumped them days before. If

6. Pierce, *Pioneer Life in Southeast Florida*, p. 162.
7. Munroe and Gilpin, *The Commodore's Story*, pp. 69–70. Evidently Commodore Munroe was being diplomatic in his description of Brickell's propensity for exaggeration. Another visitor to the bay who did not mince his words was Joseph H. Day, the uncle of J. W. Ewan and an investor in the Biscayne Bay Co.; he called Brickell "the most unmitigated liar I have ever met." See Joseph H. Day, "Diary of a Trip to Miami in 1877," in collection of the Historical Association of Southern Florida.
8. Post Office Information from the National Archives, Dade County, Florida, p. 30. Copy in files of Historical Association of Southern Florida, Miami.

the local citizens were discomfited by such procedures, they had to endure, for Alice held the post until 1889. The same take-it-or-leave-it attitude with which she approached the mail carried over into her dealings with paying customers. The citizens around the bay depended on the store for flour, salt, sugar, kerosene, groceries, and clothing items, but they often had to take what the Brickells were in a mood to sell them at a given time. Although the settlers may have learned to cope with the idiosyncrasies of the Brickells, there were too few of them in the 1870–90 period to create any great volume of business. Brickell regularly sailed his eleven-ton sloop *Ada* to Key West carrying cargo and passengers, and it was occasionally used for turtling expeditions, but it was the Seminole trade that made the family prosper.

The Seminoles would pole their dugout canoes down the Miami River, past the rapids formed by a limestone ridge that kept the salt water from intruding upstream, and pull their craft up on the bank in front of the store. They also came in from camps on Snake Creek, some ten miles farther north. In 1880 there were reportedly sixty-nine Indians living in the vicinity of Miami.[9] They brought in such items as alligator hides, alligator teeth, buckskin, egret plumes, pumpkins, sweet potatoes, gophers, and the coontie starch that was made from the wild Zamia root.[10] The value of these items fluctuated with the season and market demand, but the trade was generally profitable for Indian and storekeeper. For example, the trader could buy coontie starch for three to five cents a pound from the Seminoles and some whites who made it, then take it to Key West, where it sold for twice that amount. Alligator hides could bring several dollars each to the Indian hunter, while the reptile's teeth were worth ten cents a pound. Dressed deerskins were worth forty to fifty cents each, but buckskin dyed with red mangrove bark sold

9. Clay MacCauley, "Inhabitants in Miami River Settlement, in the County of Dade, State of Florida, Enumerated By Me On The 9th Day Of February, 1880." Copy in files of Historical Association of Southern Florida, Miami.

10. In 1885 the Brickell store was visited by Cyrus Beede, special agent sent to locate lands for the Seminoles in Florida, who reported of a rather typical trading day on the Miami River: "I noticed one canoe load of provisions brought in by the Indians, to consist of sweet potatoes, a few bananas, some starch, and a *live hog* securely tied and snugly stowed away under the front seat weighing I judge, about 100 pounds. This hog brought him six dollars, and I think he realized one dollar per bushell for the potatoes." Document 30447, Office of Indian Affairs, Correspondence Received File, November 15, 1887.

for one dollar a pound. In addition to the items sold in the store, the Seminoles supplied settlers with various food items; one woman recalls buying huckleberries for ten cents a quart and chickens for fifty cents in the 1890s.[11]

The transactions at Brickell's store were not "barter" per se, for the Seminoles received payment for each item in gold and silver coins. These in turn were used to purchase necessities such as salt, guns and ammunition, canned goods, sewing materials, and decorative items. A particular favorite among Seminole women was brightly colored beads which they wore in necklaces often stretching from "shoulder tip to ear."[12] The Indian women would not wear just any cheap trade bead, but as MacCauley reported, "They are satisfied with nothing meaner than a cut glass bead, about a quarter of an inch or more in length, generally of some shade of blue, and costing (so I was told by a trader at Miami) $1.75 a pound. Sometimes, but not often, one sees beads of inferior quality worn."[13] An archaeological survey of the Brickell trading post site within the last decade yielded samples of at least thirty different types of beads that were sold there.[14] MacCauley further noted that "these beads must be burdensome to their wearers."[15] This was purportedly borne out when one squaw was persuaded to take off her necklaces and put them on the store scale at Brickell's, and they weighed in at twenty-five pounds.

Commodore Munroe, whom Brickell transported to Biscayne for the first time in 1877, has provided one of the few first-hand accounts of the Indian trade at Miami. He recalled that "The Seminole Indians were frequent visitors to Mr. Brickell's trading store. Big Tiger, son of the old warchief, Tigertail, with his squaw and papooses, were there when we arrived—fine specimens of Indians; if the rest of the tribe were anywhere his equals, I don't wonder at the length of the two wars. Indian Charley, who had lost part of an ear for lying, and Jimmy, who was conspicuous for taking most excel-

11. Mary Douthit Conrad, "Homesteading in Florida during the 1890's," pp. 9, 14.
12. Munroe and Gilpin, The Commodore's Story, p. 101.
13. Clay MacCauley, "The Seminole Indians of Florida," pp. 487–88.
14. Robert Carr, "The Brickell Store and Seminole Trade" (typescript). This soon-to-be-published work is a report of an archaeological survey of the Brickell trading post site carried out in 1965. The final report will be issued by the Florida Department of State, Division of Archives, History, and Records Management.
15. MacCauley, "The Seminole Indians of Florida," p. 347.

lent care of his old mother, I saw later, also Chief Tigertail and Cypress Tiger . . . Mr. Brickell did a good business with them nearly every day. . . . One showed me a pair of field glasses, $15 trade, so he told me; I failed to discover anything but plain glass in them, though he seemed satisfied. Alarm clocks and hand-power sewing machines were in demand. Bright calico prints had displaced the old buckskin of their garments, which were often made up of a wide variety of colors and patterns; I have seen *fourteen* in one shirt."[16] Munroe's implication that Brickell sold the Indian shoddy merchandise is intriguing, to say the least. Most informants suggest just the opposite, that Brickell and other permanent traders had to give the Seminoles fair value to retain their business. Also, the Brickells apparently took a personal interest in the welfare of their Seminole clients in a number of ways. There is one known incident in which William Brickell wrote to protest to federal authorities when it was suspected that one of the Seminole hunters had had his venison poisoned by the keeper of the house of refuge near New River.

Miami, Fla.
June–15–91

The Indian Commissioner
Washington D.C.

Sir

On the sixth day of June Indian Charley was sailing from Hillsborough to New River when his canoe capsized, he went to Station No 4 to leave a deer that he had shot while hunting, he left it there for one night. he got the venison next day and took it to camp and cooked it for supper, all the Indians that eat any of the venison were then taken very sick so they sent Little Tiger to report. He came down and said all the Indians in one camp had been poisoned and that thirteen was sick and several they thought would die. We at once forwarded some medicine and the Indians are getting slowly better. They wish me to forward you a piece of the venison so that you can have it analized and see what the Temporary Keeper put on it.

The citizens here would like the matter looked into for it will not be safe if a stranger can come in and put poison in things the Indians have to eat.

Respectfully W. B. Brickell   Miami Fla.[17]

16. Munroe and Gilpin, *The Commodore's Story*, p. 100.
17. Letter, W. B. Brickell to Commissioner of Indian Affairs, June 15, 1891,

In the early years there was apparently a great deal of social interaction between the Seminoles and settlers in the small community at the mouth of the Miami River. It was not uncommon for the Indians to visit in the homes of their white friends, and they were generally in attendance at most civic and social functions such as weddings. A few also attended the Sunday religious services held in the garden of the Brickell home, where they reportedly enjoyed the hymn singing.[18] For their part, the Seminoles taught the settlers how to make use of many products in their new milieu: sofkee, the gruel made from the coontie flour; the bud of the cabbage palm; Indian pumpkin and guava syrup; woven products made from palmetto leaves; and turtle and manatee meat used in stews. They also served as guides for hunting parties and surveying teams which were mapping the southern end of the state. Until the coming of the railroad and the arrival of a population which looked upon them as curiosities, the Seminole people were a welcome and accepted part of community life in the frontier settlement of Miami.

Rarely was there any friction between the settlers and Seminoles, but one notable confrontation took place between Mary Brickell and the Seminole leader Big Tom Tiger. An anonymous biographer of the family described the situation: "The Government troops were stationed on the south side of Miami River. The Indians were expected to go on a rampage, so Government troops were station [sic] for protection against the Indians. Indians from all over Florida met here just south of the Brickell home. Mrs. Brickell with Maude Brickell, a tiny infant in her arms, went out and met the Indian Chief Big Tom Tiger and talked with him and explained to him Mr. Brickell was away and she was alone with the children. After a lengthy conversation the Chief promised Mrs. Brickell to go away, and never return in a war against the whites—they never fought again. Maude Brickell was rocked and petted by all the important Indians of her time. She was the first white baby that many of the Indians had ever seen. The Indians became staunch friends of the

---

Document 22617, Office of Indian Affairs, Correspondence Received File, June 25, 1891. The medical inspector for the bureau replied to Brickell on July 13, 1891, stating that the meat showed no signs of poisoning other than ptomaine. There is no official record of the reaction of the bureau employee who opened Brickell's original letter containing the venison sent from Florida.

18. Muir, Miami, U.S.A., p. 16. Commodore Munroe corroborates the view that the Seminoles were welcome visitors in homes around the bay. See The Commodore's Story, p. 101.

Brickells—came to their home for food, medical attention and advice."[19] This incident, although unverified, could have taken place some time in 1872 when the federal government was considering sending a special agent to Florida to check on reports of unrest among the Seminoles.[20]

Across the river from the Brickell store, a section of land on which Fort Dallas was located belonged to the Biscayne Bay Company before it came into Julia Tuttle's possession. The firm planned to develop the land during the 1870s; a company store was established, and the "Maama" post office reactivated, but the venture never succeeded.[21] One of the major investors in the venture sent a nephew, J. W. Ewan of Charleston, down to survey the situation. Ewan was taken with the beauty of the region and decided to remain, making his home in Fort Dallas until the Tuttle family arrived in 1891. An immensely popular man of urbane wit and charm, Ewan came to be known as the "Duke of Dade" when he served the county in the legislature. He carried on a limited trading activity with the Seminoles from the store in the fort. On a trip to the area in 1879, an observer reported that at Fort Dallas ". . . the middle room was used as a store by William Ewan. At this time Ewan was away on a trip to Key West to purchase supplies for his store. The main business he had was trading with the Indians." It was also noted that ". . . an Indian brought to the store seven hundred snowy heron plumes; they gave him twenty-five cents in trade for each plume."[22] Ewan was apparently the trader referred to by MacCauley who described one method of conducting business with the Indians during his visit in 1880:

> At Miami a trader keeps his accounts with the Indians in single marks or pencil strokes. For example, an Indian brings

19. Manuscript in files of the *Miami Herald*. Unsigned, untitled, undated. It appears that this handwritten account of the Brickell family was prepared either by one of the family members or a confidant, but not a professional journalist.

20. U.S., Congress, House, *Report of the Commissioner of Indian Affairs*, Exec. Doc. 1, 42d Cong., 3d sess., 1872, pp. 413–14. It is possible that the federal troops stationed on the south side of the Miami River had been sent there during a yellow fever outbreak at Key West in 1873. See "Reminiscences of Mrs. A. C. Richards, 1903."

21. Post Office Information from the National Archives, Dade County, Florida, p. 30. Copy in files of Historical Association of Southern Florida, Miami.

22. Pierce, *Pioneer Life in Southeast Florida*, pp. 126–27.

to him buck skins, for which the trader allows twelve "chalks." The Indian, not wishing then to purchase anything, receives a piece of paper marked in this way:

"//// //// ////
J.W.E. owes Little Tiger $3."

At his next visit the Indian may buy five "marks" worth of goods. The trader then takes the paper and returns it to Little Tiger changed as follows:

"//// ///
J.W.E. owes Little Tiger $1.75."

Thus the account is kept until all the "marks" are crossed off, when the trader takes the paper into his own possession. The value of the purchases made at Miami by the Indians, I was informed, is annually about $2,000. This is, however, an amount larger than would be the average for the rest of the tribe, for the Miami Indians do a considerable business in the barter and sale of ornamental plumage.[23]

Ewan and his Seminole patrons had evidently evolved a form of credit arrangement based upon the twenty-five cent piece, which the Indians called "kan-cat-ka-hum-him," literally translated as "one mark on the ground" in their tongue.[24] This form of credit arrangement differed from the regular account books kept by some other traders at a later time, although most preferred to deal with the Indians on a cash basis. Ewan seems to have been out of business when Pierce visited the Miami River in 1882, and his trade was apparently inherited by the Brickell store.

When the Florida East Coast Railroad came to Miami in 1896, the embryonic town on the north side of the river began to grow rapidly. A business district appeared, the population soared, and wealthy tourists came by train and yacht to winter at Flagler's fab-

23. MacCauley, "The Seminole Indians of Florida," p. 524.
24. Ibid. There is no mention in the MacCauley report of a visit to the Brickell store; thus the assumption is that his observations on the Indian trade were made at Ewan's store alone. It is interesting that the trading phrase used by the Indians there was "kan-cat-ka-hum-him" which translated as "one mark on the ground," for this appears to be a Muskogee phrase. (See W. S. Robertson and David Winslett, *Muskogee or Creek First Reader.*) The Indians who traded at Miami were Mikasuki speakers; however, it is known that the Muskogee speakers occasionally did travel as far south as the Miami River region.

ulous Royal Palm Hotel fronting on the bay and river. This was the type of progress that Julia Tuttle had envisioned and which she had devoted her energies and land to obtaining. Isolated on the south bank of the river without a bridge connecting them to the activity on the other side, the Brickells soon lost their dominant place in the commercial life of the area. When a bridge was built, it went well to the west of Brickell Point, and this completed Brickell's alienation from Henry M. Flagler. He had not liked Flagler's imperious manner when he first came to negotiate for land, prior to extending his tracks into the Miami area; then, to make matters worse, the Flagler dredges had deposited a spoil bank in front of his home, obstructing the view. The old man reportedly vowed never to cross the river again—and he probably never did. Mary Brickell was more flexible; she sold the fill to road builders, then had herself licensed as a realtor and hired agents to sell the family land that was opened when they donated right-of-way for a road from Miami to Coconut Grove. The Brickells also had extensive land holdings in the upper end of the county at New River, and these acreages would play a significant role in replenishing family coffers: later the Brickells could build a twenty-two-room mansion overlooking the bay. Yet, by the turn of the century the family had retreated to their sanctum sanctorum, and the trading days were ended forever at Brickell Point.

The new merchants who flocked into the boom town of Miami were primarily interested in catering to the townspeople and wealthy winter tourists, and though most of them dealt with the Seminoles as a matter of course, only a few could be classified as traders in the generally accepted usage of the term. From the reminiscences of these merchants one can piece together a picture of how the Indians were accepted and dealt with in the years prior to the Florida "land boom" of the 1920s. For the most part, the Seminoles, with their exotic costumes, egret plumes, and native handicrafts to sell, were viewed as a colorful addition to the tourist mecca. Amusement parks such as those at Musa Isle and in Hialeah featured "authentic" Seminole villages, and special demonstrations were often arranged for tourists at the lavish hotels. However, the products which the Indians brought in from the Everglades—pelts, plumes, and hides— became less and less important in the economy of the city. William Brickell, who died in 1908, did not live to see the dynamiting of the limestone ledge that formed the rapids of the Miami River; this event signalled the advent of a concerted effort to drain the Everglades and open the river as an artery for bringing agricultural products raised on the newly drained land to market. This drainage scheme, initiated under Governor N. B. Broward, would increasingly restrict the range of the Indians, making hunting and trapping more difficult. In addition, the passage of state and national laws protecting plume birds, the changing whims of fashion, and a renewed national conscience against the wanton destruction of certain species such as the alligator to provide leather goods, all led to a greatly diminished demand for Seminole products. Even so, the Seminoles continued to patronize Miami merchants—unfortunately, an ever increasing volume of their business went to saloon keepers—until the sheer size of the urban sprawl and lack of easy access via water ended their mass visits to the city.

Isidor Cohen, a naturalized citizen of Russian descent, came to Miami on February 6, 1896.[25] He had traveled by small steamboat from Fort Lauderdale, then the terminus of the railroad, but had had to leave his merchandise at Lemon City because there were no docking facilities at Miami. He first attempted to secure land from Julia Tuttle for a store on the north bank of the river, but having no success in this, Cohen settled on the south shore west of Brickell Point. A Key West man named Cobb who ran a saw mill agreed to provide land and material for a store, and a man named Clayton built it in four days while Cohen stayed at his home; all, of course, was done on credit. Once the young merchant was ensconced in his new store, he found, as the Brickells had, that business was slow on the south shore, so one month later he capitulated to the exorbitant rents being asked and moved into a store rented to him by the banker W. M. Brown. Within a few months the Florida East Coast tracks were laid into Miami, and business began to thrive. In his diary and memoirs, Cohen gives a pithy, first-hand account of social, political, and mercantile life in the frontier settlement. In a chapter recalling pioneers' amusements and thrills, he wrote: "Additional amusement was afforded by the periodic visits of Indians that came down the Miami River from the Everglades in canoes laden with raccoon, otter, mink and alligator hides, and often with beautiful egrets, and other rare plumes. This form of amusement proved highly profitable to some of the pioneers, especially the saloon-keepers of North Miami, who carried on a considerable traffic with the Indians. Not all Indians, however, converted their wares into

25. Isidor Cohen, *Historical Sketches and Sidelights of Miami, Fla.,* p. 13.

whiskey. Charley Tigertail, brother of Jack Tigertail, who about a year or so ago was shot and killed in the Indian village of Musa Isle, used to ship his wares direct to the northern markets and receive his returns in gold coin. He invested the proceeds of such sales in merchandise which he retailed among his own people at enormous profits."[26] Cohen also claimed to have sold the first umbrella ever retailed in Miami to Charley Tigertail, "who also bought a suit of clothes, a derby hat and a red bandana and wore the complete outfit back to the Everglades, using the umbrella as a walking stick."[27] Nowhere in his accounts is there any mention of being able to sell shoes to a Seminole.

Near the end of his reminiscences, published in 1925, Isidor Cohen was already regretting the passing of many of the interesting people and the simpler way of life that had made Miami so attractive in its early years. "The Seminole Indians," he wrote, "who had been very much in evidence in the early days of Miami are now rarely seen on the streets of the city except during the tourist season when they appear in groups of gaudily dressed men, women and children and receive much attention from the winter visitors. They also derive considerable revenue from visitors to their villages, which are located in the northwestern sections of the city at Musa Isle, overlooking the north fork of the Miami River, and at Hialeah, to whom they sell Indian souvenirs. . . . Their number, however, is fast diminishing. They are a peaceable people and were always great favorites with Miami's pioneers. An intoxicated Indian is an extremely rare sight, whereas in the early days a sober one was just as rare. The partial drainage of the Everglades and its penetration by the whites have deprived the red man of his heritage, namely, the game which that vast territory harbored in great abundance. Despite their precarious existence they stubbornly resist Uncle Sam's efforts to remove them to a western Indian reservation where they would become wards of the government. They evidently love their independence too well to exchange it for ease and comfort."[28] Although Cohen, like most whites, harbored a skewed perception of the life of "ease and comfort" which Indians led on a reservation, he was not mistaken about their love of independence. But how was the Seminole to be

26. Ibid., pp. 27–28. For further information on Tigertail's trading ventures see Tebeau, *Florida's Last Frontier*, p. 55; Alason B. Skinner, "The Florida Seminoles," p. 162.
27. E. C. Nance, ed., *The East Coast of Florida*, 3:438.
28. Cohen, *Historical Sketches*, pp. 204–5.

independent when the land and his major means of livelihood were being denied him? The income from the tourist camp which some turned to in desperation was hardly a fair exchange for a loss of self-respect and the demeaning aspect of becoming a public exhibition; moreover, the lack of public drunkenness which Cohen found laudable was probably attributable to the drinking being confined to the tourist traps or to camps away from the downtown Miami area. This lack of true independence might have become the fate of more of the tribe had it not been for the establishment of federal reservations in Florida, and the gradual turning of the Seminoles to cattle raising and other domestic pursuits starting in the 1930s.

In 1898, William M. Burdine moved his family down from Bartow and established a small mercantile business, W. M. Burdine and Sons, in a 25-by-50-foot frame building on South Miami Avenue between Flagler and First Streets. The family did business at that location for fourteen years until they moved into their new five-story building in 1912; at that time it was the largest structure south of Jacksonville. During the early years of the store, the Seminole Indians "sold their alligator and otter hides down the street, then came to William Burdine to buy vests and heavy gold watch chains, derby hats, and ostrich plumes to adorn their chieftain's turbans, and colorful calico for their clothes." Burdine was fond of his Indian customers and often used terms from their language which most white Miamians knew in his newspaper advertisement: "We have them *ojus* and no humbug. We make no claim to sell goods at cost all the time, but when we announce a special bargain sale, it means something."[29]

Although there have been accounts which claimed that buyers from the store purchased plumes directly from hunters in the Everglades, this cannot be conclusively affirmed. G. E. Whitten began working part-time in the original Burdine store while he was in high school and joined the firm as a clerk and bookkeeper in 1913; ultimately he became president and chairman of the board. He can recall no time that Burdines engaged in the plume trade either buying or selling, although Indians did frequent the store for this purpose. He remembers that when the Seminoles came to town they "would usually go to J. D. Girtman's grocery store and buy all their groceries, then they would come to Burdines and buy their calico for

29. Advertisement for "Burdine's 1898 store" celebration. Provided by Burdine's, courtesy of Mr. G. E. Whitten.

their costumes. Quite often they would bring in egrets that they tried to sell, and did sell, and made money which they paid for their merchandise and the liquor that they bought." They came in two or three times a month and "sat on the floor at the rear of the store . . . as tourists would come to the store from the Royal Palm Hotel particularly, they would try to sell them egrets. . . .I think they were selling them anywhere from $5 to $7.50, whatever they could get out of them."[30] After Burdines moved into its new store, the Indian business began to fade appreciably, and Whitten does not recall any Indians coming in large groups after the 1920s.

Although the Burdines were not, strictly speaking, traders, i.e., they did not engage in a reciprocal buying and selling relationship with the Seminoles, nevertheless the Indian business was welcomed and viewed as an asset both to the income and image of the establishment. In later years, W. M. Burdine, Jr. spent much time on his ranch in central Florida, where Indians hunted and worked cattle for the family, and one Seminole family even named their child Willie Burdine. Like many other children of trading families, Burdine had formed his first impressions and attachments to the Seminoles while they were doing business with his father.

A block and a half away from Burdine's store, at Avenue D and Eleventh Street, was located the original Girtman Grocery Store. This was the acknowledged center of Seminole trading activity in Miami after the turn of the century, and the Girtman family has left a vivid account of their dealings with the Indians in their early store and at a later Flagler Avenue location.[31] James D. Girtman was born in Georgia, but came to Orange County, Florida, as a boy, his father having moved there to plant a citrus grove in the early 1880s. The Girtman family remained in their grove home near Orlando until the big freeze of 1894 wiped out their holdings. The senior Girtman then moved his wife, two sons, and a daughter to newly-settled Miami, as other displaced citrus people from the central part of the state were doing. The railroad had arrived and had a large force of men working, the Royal Palm Hotel was in operation, and new people were arriving each day. It appeared to be a good place to start again, so Girtman began a grocery store, with his two sons

30. Interview with Mr. George E. Whitten, Miami, October 8, 1972. Tape and transcript in University of Florida Indian Oral History Archives, Florida State Museum, Gainesville.
31. Manuscript of interview with Mr. J. D. Girtman, Miami, December 10, 1938. Typescript in the Florida Collection, University of South Florida.

working as clerks. However, there were four other grocery stores already established in the town, and the railroad brought in all of the supplies for the hotel and operated its own commissary for the workers and their families. There was not enough business for five stores, so the Girtmans decided to convert their business to a "trading post" catering primarily to the Seminoles who came in from the Everglades. The elder Girtman died in 1910, and J. D. then took over the management of the family store.

A pioneer of Miami, Hoyt Frazure, has provided a description of the Indian traffic which arrived at the city and insight into their affection for the Girtmans. "As many as 20 canoes were often pulled up at a landing in the Miami River at the foot of NW First Street. It was something to see, a string of dugout canoes coming down the river, each with a brave, dressed in colorful garb, standing in the stern and wielding a guiding pole in his hands. The arrangement of the family in each canoe was always the same—the squaw sitting forward, the children and the family's possessions occupying the middle. In the bow was the family's dog, standing there alert, his tongue hanging out the side of his mouth, ready to jump ashore as soon as the canoe touched land and set up his guard. These dogs guarded the canoes faithfully while the families went uptown to shop. I liked to watch an Indian family walk down the street, always in single file, with the father in front, followed by the boys according to age, then the mother, and after the mother, the girls. They gathered in Jimmie Girtman's store on West Flagler Street, opposite where the Miami Industrial Bank is now located. Mr. Girtman was very popular with the Indians, and they named their children after him. I remember such names as Girtman Jimmie, and also Billy Girtman, Girtman Billy, and Osceola Girtman."[32]

One well might ask what type of man could inspire such confidence among the Indians who came to trade at the store. In a 1938 interview, J. D. Girtman expanded on his business and personal involvement with the Seminoles. Primarily, the Indians brought in alligator and otter hides, diamond terrapin, plumes, and an occasional skunk or coon pelt. These they exchanged for commodities or cash according to their needs of the moment. While this was the normal pattern of trading with Indians, at Girtman's a more personal dimension was added to the transactions. In trading with Indians it was often necessary, he felt, to buy from them something worthless, such

32. Hoyt Frazure, *Memories of Old Miami*, p. 14.

as a pelt out of season or one in poor condition. It was advisable to take what they brought, even though useless, because the Indians expected it; moreover, one never knew when they would bring in something valuable. To keep their good will, Girtman related, he would frequently pay for something, then tell the Indian to take it over to a waste box and dispose of it. On one occasion an Indian brought in a dozen diamond terrapin; Girtman had no market for them, although they would have been worth two dollars each in New York had he known where to send them. He gave the Seminole the two dollars, then had him go down to the river and turn them loose. The Indian took his money and disposed of the terrapin as directed. It took Girtman two weeks to make the proper contact in New York, but then when he could sell the terrapin, the Indians seldom brought any more into the store. Nevertheless, if he had not bought those terrapin, he felt, he would have lost the confidence and friendship of the Seminoles. That was important to J. D. Girtman.

The goods which the Seminoles bought from Girtman were mostly foodstuffs such as canned meat and fish, sweets, especially jellies, syrup, molasses, cookies, sweet breads and cakes, fresh and smoked meats, especially corned beef and sausage, rice, grits, cornmeal, macaroni, spaghetti, and dried beans. Items such as soft drinks, ice cream cones, and candy were not always available at the Girtman store; the closest substitute for an ice-cold soda was ice brought in on special railroad cars and shaved to resemble snow by a special machine. A glass was filled with this "snow," and a fruit syrup was poured over it. This was the only type of soft drink available, and it was popular with both whites and Indians. The Girtmans would not handle liquor, so if the Indians wanted "Wyomee," they had to go to a local saloon. Usually one Indian would stay sober while the others were drinking so that he could get them all back to camp. Of course, the caretaker would take his liquor back to camp.

Girtman sold the Seminole women great quantities of cloth, thread, and beads used in making their colorful costumes. He did not, however, deal in sewing machines. At first, the Seminoles had no special liking for color, he recalled, and used more black to emphasize the design of their work than did other Indians. Their designs were of no special tribal or religious significance, such as with the western Indians, but were a matter of personal preference. The beads which they used in making necklaces were not suitable for use in weaving designs into the fabric, but the drygoods stores such as Girtman's in Miami and Stranahan's in Fort Lauderdale always carried a large stock of seed beads that were used for bead weaving, as well as the larger string of beads. In addition, the stores carried dyes which the Indians could buy to color their cloth, rather than making dyes from vegetable sources. Then cotton cloth began to come in bright colors such as turkey red, indigo blue, yellow, and green, and the Indians bought it by the yard. The stores also began to carry items such as bias fold, rickrack, edgings, and other trimmings so the Indian women had to depend less and less on highly intricate sewing to achieve their clothing designs.

At the time Girtman was in business, the Seminoles made little handicraft work for the tourist trade, and most "Indian" items being sold came from commercial factories or club groups. Also, the Seminoles had little in the way of authentic folk art other than their colorful clothing. Since the days of trading with the Spanish and then the English, they had been able to obtain practically everything they needed, from blankets to firearms, kettles, and other hardware. The arts of pottery and basketry had been lost almost completely, and the same was true of metal work; about the only metal decorative ornaments that the Seminoles wore were the bracelets made of pierced silver and gold coins and a few other pieces of hand-hammered work described by Goggin.[33]

In the old days, on rainy or cold nights, the Girtman store would be full of Indians who made their beds on the floor, and the door was locked until morning. In fact, Girtman built an addition to his trading post where he kept extra stock and where the Seminoles could have a sleeping place. The Indians made it their headquarters when they came to Miami. In those days Girtman considered the Indians to be honest and truthful and trusted them to be on his premises without supervision. The Indians returned his kindness in naming children after the family, in bringing gifts, and in having Girtman as an honored guest at their annual Green Corn Dance. However, as the years passed, the storekeeper saw a progressive decline in the independence and self-respect of the Indians who came to his store, and he blamed this on a commercialization of the Seminoles in tourist camps and increased alcohol consumption; both of these conditions accelerated with the decline of the good hunting and trapping conditions in the Everglades.

The Girtman store figured prominently in one of the most highly

33. John M. Goggin, "Silver Work of the Florida Seminole," pp. 25–32.

publicized cases of a white man victimizing an Indian in the early years of this century. The case involved the notorious Ashley Gang —a family of bank robbers and moonshiners who operated along the lower east coast of Florida until the 1920s. On December 9, 1911, a digger dredge working on the canal between Fort Lauderdale and Lake Okeechobee churned up the body of a Seminole identified as DeSoto Tiger. A friend of the dead man, Jimmy Gopher, reported that the Indian was last seen in the company of John Ashley. Investigation brought out the fact that the two had started down the canal with a load of otter skins which John alone had sold later to Girtman Brothers in Miami for $1,200.[34] Ashley was arrested and finally tried and convicted of the murder, but through quirks of the law, he was imprisoned a short time for the lesser crime of bank robbery. Ultimate retribution came when, on November 1, 1924, the Ashley Gang came to a blazing end in a gun battle with sheriff's deputies on the Sebastian River Bridge.

Girtman sold out his business in 1915. He saw that the old trading days were over. The Indians could no longer bring in pelts or plumes, and the drainage had made the use of their boats near Miami impossible; they had to walk to get to the city. He did a large credit business with his "friends," giving canned food, dry-goods, and other things they asked for and charging them on the books. They intended to pay sometime, and he believed that they would have paid had he remained in business long enough. When he closed his store, he had $6,000 in outstanding accounts which his "friends" considered canceled because there was no longer a store to do business with. Yet, as late as the 1930s they would still occasionally bring a duck or a fish, wanting twice what it was worth; perhaps, like other things he used to buy, it was worthless, but Girtman would purchase it and the Indian would say "good friend" and then go on his way. In many ways it was a sad epilogue to the trading days of a proud people.

34. Hix G. Stuart, *The Notorious Ashley Gang*, p. 9.

3

Stranahan and Company
On the New River

Frank Stranahan was twenty-eight years of age when he arrived at the New River on January 31, 1893, and became the first permanent white resident of the settlement later to be called Fort Lauderdale. He had come to manage the overnight camp and ferry crossing on the overland stagecoach route between Lantana and Lemon City which had replaced the "Barefoot Mailman" trail along the beaches. A native of Vienna, Ohio, Stranahan had impaired his health working in the steel mills around Youngstown and came south seeking a more equable climate, as well as economic opportunity. In the late 1880s he settled in Melbourne, and for a number of years he worked in the store owned by E. P. Branch and E. C. Thomas, learning a great deal about the mercantile business in the process. When a county road was completed from the south end of Lake Worth to the Miami area in 1892, the Bay Biscayne Hack Line was formed and acquired the mail contract; a ferry was established at New River with Edward Moffatt in charge, while Capt. William Valentine served as postmaster.[1] Later, Frank Stranahan was hired to go down and start the overnight camp, but he ultimately took over the other operations as well.

In a letter to his brother William, written on the day of his arrival, Stranahan described his new situation and the wild beauty of the New River region: "One week ago to night [sic] I left Melbourne. Here I am in camp . . . at present, I have most of the say, or sort of

1. Philip Weidling and August Burghard, *Checkered Sunshine, the History of Fort Lauderdale 1793–1955*, pp. 14, 16, 31.

act Supt. . . . Have the tents, all have floors in and furnished equal
to any hotel. . . . After day work today cook sat under his tent with
gun and killed 4 gray squirrels, all we wanted for couple of meals,
coots, ducks, all kinds of fish, Tarpon or silver King. . . . Manatee or
sea cow weight from 500 lb. to 800 lb. Porpoises, Sharks, Wild cats,
Otter, Deer, Alligators all the game any one wants. . . . The Indians
here are Seminoles and talk very good English I think I will get
along with them all right."[2] This last statement proved prophetic,
for within a short time, Stranahan began what was to become a very
lucrative trade with the Seminoles.

There had been Seminole camps on the New River for many
years, and an early hunting visitor to the area, Charles Cory, has left
a rich account of how the Indians hunted and trapped their game.
Cory's book was published in 1896, but he had been hunting in
Florida intermittently since the 1870s and knew the Seminoles quite
well. In describing the territory, he wrote, "New River (New-la-pee)
flows east and enters into New River Sound, which, in turn, opens
into the ocean five miles farther to the south. New River is very deep
in places and is one of the best localities on the coast for manatee.
It is the favorite hunting ground of the Indians when they desire to
kill one of these animals. Several of the Indians have permanent
camps on New River. Tom Tiger, Robert Osceola, Jumper, Old Tom,
Old Charlie, and Tom-a-luske all have camps there."[3] He noted that
manatees "live equally in salt or fresh water, and while with the
Indians on one of their manatee hunts I have seen half a dozen
rising to the surface of the ocean at one time, over a quarter of a
mile from shore. . . . These animals come to the surface every few
minutes to breathe, and their heads may be seen as they appear for
a moment above the surface of the water. . . . They harpoon them
as they rise to the surface, using a steel point barbed on one side,
attached to the end of a long pole. To the steel point is fastened
a strong cord, which in turn is attached to a float. Upon being struck
the manatee sinks at once, but the direction in which he moves is
indicated by the float. The Indians follow the float as closely as
possible and watch for him to rise to the surface, when they shoot

2. Letter, Frank Stranahan to Will Stranahan, Jan. 31, 1893. Unless otherwise indicated all letters cited in this chapter are in the collection of the Historical Society of Fort Lauderdale.
3. Charles B. Cory, *Hunting and Fishing in Florida,* pp. 96–97; James A.
Henshall, *Camping and Cruising in Florida.*

him through the head, and the huge animal is then towed to shore."[4]
The animal was then skinned out and the meat shared among the
hunters for use in stews, and some was given to their white friends.

There was no commercial value to the manatee or to the Florida
brown bear; nevertheless, "the Indians were very fond of bear meat
and extract an oil from the fat which they prize highly. Whenever
a bear is discovered a hunting party is immediately organized and
the animal is tracked to his hiding place, surrounded and killed."[5]
Deer abounded in the South Florida region and were often hunted
both for food and trade. "When deer hunting the Indians divide into
small parties, two or three bucks hunting together, taking with them
their squaws and children. . . . When in the vicinity of a white settlement they find a ready market for their venison and what they do
not sell is smoked and dried for future use; dried venison will keep
very well, but it is tough and impalatable."[6] One hunting technique
of the Seminoles which often brought them into conflict with the
white settlers in more populated areas was the practice of burning
the scrub to drive out game. "The Indians burn the country every
spring in a most reckless manner, destroying great quantities of
timber. They set the dry grass on fire, so that, by destroying the old
grass, the new, fresh shoots coming up attract the deer and turkeys
which are generally found on such places. Besides this, the ground
being burned off renders still-hunting much more easy, for the game
can then be so much more readily seen. The Indians are splendid
hunters, but few of them can beat a white man shooting at a mark.
I have seen Osceola kill a deer while running at full speed, nearly
a hundred yards distant; I have also seen him drop two deer, one
after the other, before the second one had time to run, and on another occasion I saw him miss a fox-squirrel on the top of a tree
three times in succession."[7] It should be noted that in the years before the Seminoles were able to trade for modern rifles, their weapons, many of which dated back to the Seminole Wars, left a great
deal to be desired in accuracy over distance.

By the 1890s, it was apparent that "the Indians kill a great many
alligators for the purpose of selling their skins to traders. As a rule
they 'fire hunt' them at night. The alligator, lying with his eyes out

4. Cory, Hunting and Fishing, pp. 24–25.
5. Ibid., p. 27.
6. Ibid.
7. Ibid., p. 29.

of the water, does not appear to be afraid of the light which is reflected in his eye, having the appearance of a brillant candle flame,
and may be seen for a considerable distance. The Indian paddling
in his canoe approaches within a few feet of the animal and easily
shoots him through the head, after which he is speared and towed
to shore. . . . Thousands are killed annually in this manner, and
their skins are shipped North or sold to intermediate dealers in
Jacksonville and vicinity at the rate of ten cents per running foot."[8]

Near the end of his narrative, Cory indicates that "three miles
south from Snook Creek by the county road we reach New River,
where one finds a comfortable camp owned by Mr. Frank Stranahan,
and usually passengers bound for Biscayne Bay stop over night at
this point."[9] Cory was obviously not aware that the camp belonged
to the hack line and that Stranahan only served as its manager.
Nevertheless, Frank Stranahan was an ambitious man, and the
profit to be made in supplying pelts and hides from the region to
meet a growing demand for these products was not lost on his en-

8. Ibid., pp. 27, 69. See also Kirk Munroe, "Alligator Hunting with Seminoles," pp. 576–81.

9. Cory, *Hunting and Fishing*, p. 96. Midway between New River and the
settlements on Lake Worth lay the small community of Linton, founded in 1895
by a group from Michigan. One of the first settlers, Henry Sterling, built a
commissary to serve the farming families and Seminole Indians who frequently
stopped there when they were hunting in the area. The Indians were welcome
because they brought fresh venison and other food items which the settlers
used. Often the Indians stayed overnight, camping near the two-story building
where the Sterlings had their commissary with living quarters above. One such
visit proved memorable for Mrs. Sterling and her young daughter Ethel, both
of whom had just arrived from the North. It was 1896, and a kitchen had been
added to the side of the Sterling's building. On the mail-order stove was a
bright new pot, and a shiny big spoon hung beside it on the wall. Suddenly a
Seminole appeared in the doorway, pointed to the utensils, and said "Me want.
. . . bring back with sun," The mother and daughter, alone at the time, were
stunned speechless, and quite shaken. However, the next morning when Mrs.
Sterling went down to the kitchen she found both items, clean and shiny, in
their places.

Ethel Sterling Williams well remembers the buying habits of the Seminoles
who visited her father's commissary. "They just pointed to what they wanted
in our catalog and said they would return in so many moons to get their
merchandise through trade. . . . Once the Indians found a hand organ, like one
used with the monkey and tin cup, and ordered that." Her parents thought
it a strange request, but ordered it anyway. Unfortunately, the Indian never
returned to claim it! The Seminoles were a common sight around the community well after it grew to town size and was renamed Delray in 1901. For
further information see Cecil W. and Margoann Farrar, *Incomparable Delray
Beach . . . its early Life and Lore* (Boynton Beach, Fla., 1974), pp. 16–17; *Palm
Beach Post-Times*, August 18, 1974, p. 8B.

trepreneurial mind. He began to buy some items from the Indians for resale and shipped them out via Lantana; however, a sustained profit was to be made only by establishing a permanent, volume trading outlet for the Seminoles.

The first step in establishing this position, Stranahan became convinced, was to build and stock a store at the New River camp. However, land prices were high and Stranahan did not have ready capital to buy building materials and supplies, so he sought an association with an established businessman who was interested in the possibility of profitable trading with the Seminoles and settlers. By May of 1893 he had entered into an arrangement with F. M. Welles of Boston, Massachusetts, who also had other business interests in Florida. The venture was launched when Welles wrote, "I sent you from Banyan 1 case containing scale, scoop, box starch, 200 empty shells, #12 ½ keg FFF G. powder (which had been opened), pkge primers, some cans of salmon, etc. all being things I had there and could spare. I have also left word for a part of a bbl. syrup & part bbl. vinegar to be shipped to you from there."[10] Welles was also to serve as the factor in marketing pelts and alligator hides which Stranahan received from the Indians, and he wrote from Jacksonville, "I can sell here in Jax. any hides or skins you are likely to buy but hope to get better prices offered for them in N.Y. Gator skins are low—can only get here from 10 to 80¢ for 'green salted' according to size of from 3 ft. up. Indian *dressed* deer skins I am offered abt. $1 per lb., for cow hides 3 to 4½¢ lb. I can sell all kinds of skins or furs, beeswax, tallow, 'Gator teeth, live gators, etc, I think."[11]

Welles had also made arrangements to have a stock of goods and building materials for the store shipped from Jacksonville on the schooner *Reynolds,* and urged Stranahan to complete the surveying and purchase of land at New River. A $300 line of credit was also arranged for Stranahan at the Indian River State Bank of Titusville. Apparently the partnership was off to an auspicious start, but disaster struck when the ship loaded with their goods wrecked, with a total loss of cargo. The combination of this financial loss and continued difficulties in getting supplies to the isolated New River camp led the two men to dissolve their association early in 1894.[12] At that

10. Letter, F. M. Welles to Frank Stranahan, May 4, 1893.
11. Ibid., May 6, 1893.
12. Ibid., Apr. 6, 1894.

point Stranahan turned to other businessmen in the South Florida
area to help underwrite his venture.

Stranahan was able to purchase ten acres of land from William
and Mary Brickell on the condition that he move the camp and his
trading post some seven-tenths of a mile to the west of its original
location in Cooley Hammock, thus bringing the road through the
Brickell holdings and opening them for settlement.[13] This was the
first of many land purchases which would eventually make Frank
Stranahan one of the wealthiest men in the region. With the backing
of a number of silent partners, the firm STRANAHAN & COMPANY
was opened in a one-story frame building set a few yards back from
a wooden bulkhead and dock on the New River. The firm did business at this location until 1901, when Stranahan moved the trading
post to the ground floor of a new home built on the same tract of
land. The firm's stationery and business cards, sporting a letterhead
impression of a Seminole Indian watching a schooner entering a
palm-fringed waterway, listed Frank Stranahan as president, W. O.
Berryhill as secretary, and M. B. Lyman as treasurer. The cards also
noted that the company functioned as "dealers in general merchandise, farming utensils, crate material and paper, buyers of alligator
skins and furs."[14]

The presence of M. B. Lyman's name on the STRANAHAN &
COMPANY stationery is one of the few tangible evidences of his
role in the firm, although surviving members of the Lyman family
recall that the Lyman brothers owned at least 50 per cent of the
business in its early years.[15] The Lymans were one of the earliest
families to settle on Lake Worth, coming there in the late 1880s.
M. K. Lyman took up a homestead, while his sons, Morris Benson
Lyman and George R. Lyman, began to trade with the Indians and
other settlers from their store located on a dock at Lantana. The
store and post office were managed by M.B. (always called "Benson"
by his friends), while George captained the family schooner on
which they brought in supplies from Jacksonville and other Florida

13. Weidling and Burghard, *Checkered Sunshine*, pp. 16–17.
14. Business card and stationery of Stranahan & Company. In the collection
of the Historical Society of Fort Lauderdale.
15. Interview with Mr. Ralph Lyman, Lantana, Oct. 25, 1972. Tape and
transcript in University of Florida Indian Oral History Archives, Florida State
Museum, Gainesville. For additional information on the Lyman family, see
the series of articles appearing in the *Palm Beach Post*, May 16–19, 1962.
See also Charles W. Pierce, *Pioneer Life in Southeast Florida*, pp. 182–83,
200, 211–12.

ports. The Lymans supplied settlers living in the vicinity of lower Lake Worth and did a brisk trade with the Seminoles. It was common practice during the pioneer days in South Florida to utilize goods washed up on shore from wrecks at sea; after one such salvaging operation, the Lymans recovered several casks of Spanish wine which played a significant role in their dealing with the Indians. They placed the hogshead and a dipper on the trail leading to the store and told the Indians that after they had completed their trading they were welcome to take all the wine they desired; needless to say, this often led to some prolonged revelry. The Lymans were well-regarded and trusted by the Seminole people, and always made a point of providing a market for their pelts and hides. It is quite logical that the Lymans, operating the closest store to the New River camp, would be the ones that Stranahan turned to initially after his ill-fated venture with F. M. Welles. There are few records of transactions between the two stores—some isolated bits of correspondence between Stranahan and George Lyman and a discounted bill[16]—and the Lyman involvement was reportedly terminated as soon as Stranahan was able to buy out their interest, which almost certainly took place before the Florida East Coast Railroad arrived at New River in 1896.

Stranahan's enterprises prospered, especially his trade with the Indians, and he felt financially secure enough to take a wife. The lady in his life was young Ivy Julia Cromartie, who had come to the settlement to be its first school teacher.[17] A one-room school house had been erected, and twelve students were located to meet the Dade County minimum of nine pupils per school, but Ivy Cromartie taught only one year prior to their marriage on August 16, 1900. The following year, Stranahan built an imposing two-story structure on the river, which would serve as both trading post and family home. This building still stands, and with its high ceilings, broad verandas, and sweeping view of the New River, it is an outstanding example of Florida frontier architecture.

The Stranahans were among the staunchest friends of the Seminoles in South Florida, and both were trusted explicitly by the Indians who often traveled great distances to trade there. The win-

16. Letter, George Lyman to Frank Stranahan, June 13, 1894. Also, an invoice to Frank Stranahan on M. B. Lyman stationery, Jan. 25, 1894.
17. August Burghard, *Watchie-Esta/Hutrie (The Little White Mother)*, passim.

ter season was the heavy trading period, and Mrs. Stranahan recalled seeing as many as a hundred canoes coming down the river, loaded with Indian families, their trade goods, cookware, and animals, headed for a rendezvous at the trading post. These large groups might come in as often as every six weeks, depending upon the supply of game and where they were hunting. There were also Indian families, such as Johnny Jumper's camp, living nearby; they traded at the store and did not stay as long. Those Seminole families who came would generally stay four days to a week, camping on the grounds and keeping their dugouts in a slough which ran off the main river course. Stranahan also built a shelter with canvas roof and siding which served as a dormitory for visiting Seminoles. Often the Indians would end their visit by taking the stagecoach (later the train) to West Palm Beach for a drinking bout at Zapp's or other saloons in the vicinity; on such occasions Stranahan usually prevailed upon them to leave their weapons with him at the store until they returned to the Everglades.[18]

The Seminoles brought a variety of items to trade at Stranahan's store, according to a study by Craig and McJunkin: "After abolition of the egret plume trade in 1901, otter pelts became the most valuable trade item with a single skin priced from $7 to $8 during the winter season. . . . In summer, alligator hides brought $1.80 to $2.00 for specimens 6 to 8 feet long, but only 50 to 75 cents each for smaller hides. Newly hatched alligator eggs were also important. The Indians would place moist leaves around eggs and hatch them at the store for Stranahan who in turn sold them to tourists for 25 cents to $1.00 each, depending upon size. Garden produce in the form of corn, pumpkins (of the special Seminole variety), and beans were often offered to the store as were huckleberries and wild grapes. But the old custom of bartering preserved quail, doves, parakeets or live turkeys seems to have died out, although deerskins remained a common trade item. Kunti (koonti, compte) the famous Seminole starch and famine food, constituted a significant item of commerce at Stranahan's store. . . ."[19] The scope of the trading activities was such that some Indian groups "brought in as much as

18. Alan Craig and David McJunkin, "Stranahan's: Last of the Seminole Trading Posts," p. 48. Actually, Stranahan's was not the last of the Indian trading posts, as this study reveals.

19. Ibid. The article fails to note that if Stranahan did trade in plumes prior to his marriage, this practice came to an abrupt end, since Mrs. Stranahan was an avid Audubon Society member.

$1200 to $1500 in materials to be sold to Stranahan, although generally the amount involved was much less, usually $50–$75. In total, the Seminole trading volume was of a substantial nature, adding a significant amount to the economy of South Florida."[20]

Stranahan's store provided the Indians with practically every item necessary to survival in the Everglades wilderness during their long stays away from the trading posts. With the money received for their goods, "Seminoles bought new pots and pans, traps, good quality shotguns, ammunition, an occasional rifle, 'books' of calico (this is a 10-yard bolt folded so as to resemble pages of a book), some canned goods (particularly peaches), flour, a small amount of grits, much salt (for salting alligator hides), jewelry in general (especially watches, fobs, and beads), axes, hatchets, saws, knives, hammers, and large amounts of nails. This latter commodity was extensively used in the construction of their chickees and other structures. In addition to lard and butter used for cooking oil, they bought canned milk. Kerosene was not used for cooking but rather for illumination and as a mosquito repellant. Cheesecloth was purchased for mosquito netting. Chewing tobacco, pipes, and snuff were not popular with the clientele of Stranahan's store, but they did buy cut tobacco and cigarettes in quantity. . . . Stranahan refused to sell patent medicines, vanilla extract, or any other item containing alcohol."[21] This is indicative of the high principles which governed Stranahan in all of his dealings with the Seminoles.

Mrs. Stranahan often recounted her experiences in befriending the Seminoles early in this century.[22] For the first year or so the Indian children would not come near the white woman at the trading post, but ultimately a rapport was established and the small Seminoles roamed the Stranahan house freely during their visits. At this point Mrs. Stranahan felt that it was her Christian duty to work with the youngsters so that they might be better prepared to cope with the ever-encroaching white culture. Shunning traditional school materials such as the Webster blue back speller and McGuffey readers, she used large, brightly colored religious posters supplied by the Presbyterian Church. These posters contained pictures of saints, apostles, and other scriptural figures with their names printed under-

20. Ibid.
21. Ibid., pp. 45, 49.
22. Burghard, *Watchie-Esta/Hutrie,* passim. See also Harry A. Kersey, Jr., "Educating the Seminole Indians of Florida, 1879–1970," pp. 18–19.

neath. The Seminole children learned their letters by examining such materials as they gathered on the Stranahan's back porch or around her Model-T Ford when she drove to nearby camps. Her educational efforts were not always well received. "The parents frowned upon education," she recalled, and the "Medicine Men detested it."[23] Therefore, she concentrated on the children and did not attempt to change their elders' mode of living. Moreover, she realized that the ways of the white men were not necessarily best for Indians, and she always told the children "we don't want to make you like us. We just want to give you education, so that you can make the best of what you are."[24] Despite the resistance of some tribal elders and the hardships involved, Mrs. Stranahan continued her informal teaching for over twenty-five years, ceasing only when a federal day school was opened on the Dania Seminole Reservation in 1927.[25]

In addition to these educational efforts, there were many other instances where the Stranahans helped introduce new elements into Seminole culture. For example, Mrs. Stranahan possessed an 1893 upright sewing machine which her husband had purchased directly from the manufacturer, Thomas H. White, a yachting visitor to the area. The Indians learned to sew on this machine, and Stranahan later sold them smaller hand-cranked models ($30) to carry back to the Everglades camps; he always kept a few treadle models for them to use when visiting his store.[26] The Stranahan phonograph and wax cylinder records both amused and frightened the Indians. The Seminoles enjoyed the music but were alarmed at the talking voices, and one buck reportedly gathered up his family and commanded: "Go! No like canned man."[27] The Indians had become increasingly fond of canned goods, and this fellow apparently believed that a person was incarcerated in the cylinder like the beef and vegetables.

In 1906 Stranahan moved his business, by then called the STRAN-AHAN MERCANTILE CO., to a location on Brickell Avenue and North River Drive which was adjacent to the Florida East Coast Railroad; the riverfront home now known as "pioneer house" had seen the last of the Indian trade. One of the more profitable Stran-

23. *Fort Lauderdale News,* Sept. 29, 1968, p. 2F.
24. Ibid.
25. Roy Nash, "Survey of the Seminole Indians of Florida," p. 70.
26. *Fort Lauderdale News,* Aug. 6, 1956, p. 7.
27. Ibid.

ahan ventures early in this century was selling baby alligators to novelty shops, primarily in Jacksonville. It was reported that he would buy as many as 5,000 alligator eggs at one time from the Seminoles, paying a nickel each, then hatching them for the tourist trade.[28] One of his largest known orders came from OSKYS in Jacksonville for "three thousand at $125.00 per thousand or half that amount at $250.00 thousand,"[29] or approximately 12½¢ to 16½¢ each. The company ledgers reveal that the Seminoles continued a brisk trade with Stranahan until he sold his interests to the Oliver brothers in 1912.[30]

The ledger book and sales slips for the period 1906–11 provide a fairly accurate record of the Indians who were trading in the Fort Lauderdale area and tend to confirm the idea that the Seminoles spread their business among all of the traders in the region. The account books also offer a glimpse of social history. Among the more fascinating entries was a ledger page for "Old Charlie," followed by one for "Old Charlie's Old Squaw" and, somewhat surreptitiously, a few pages later on for "Old Charlie's Young Squaw."[31] In the increasingly monogomous Seminole society of that day, assuming responsibility for the debts of two squaws certainly marked "Old Charlie" as a man of distinction. As was their custom, the Indians honored their friends by adopting English surnames or naming their children after them; thus, it was not surprising to find an account for "Little Stranahan" on the books.

Following his retirement from the company, Stranahan devoted his remaining years to private and civic affairs. Nevertheless, during these years he maintained close relationships with the Indians and often accompanied federal officials on their visits to the camps. There were also countless instances when Stranahan ventured out alone to aid Indians who needed a friend. As Roy Nash noted, "many of his neighbors wondered why Frank Stranahan kept a horse long after the automobile had relegated most stables to the past. Few knew of his trips in the dead of night with that old horse to bury some Indian baby or friend who had died in the camps on the edge of town. The Seminole can still count to-day as a heavy

28. Ibid., July 28, 1953. Typed copy in collection of the Historical Society of Fort Lauderdale.
29. Letter, Osky's to Frank Stranahan, Sept. 8, 1910.
30. E. C. Nance, ed., *The East Coast of Florida*, 3:580, 598.
31. Ledger of Stranahan Mercantile Company, 1906–11. Ledger in collection of the Historical Society of Fort Lauderdale.

asset the interest of many stanch friends."[32] Ten times Stranahan served on the city council or city commission, and four times he was the council president. Unfortunately, many of his interests fell victim to the bust following the Florida "land boom" of the 1920s. In February of 1928 the Fort Lauderdale Bank and Trust Co. was forced to close; as one of its directors, Stranahan was forced to pay an assessment on stock owned to help defray the loss. Aside from his personal losses, Stranahan was disconsolate over the ruin of many of his friends. When the hurricane of May, 1929, brought further disaster to the local economy, Frank Stranahan took his own life by tying roof tiles to his waist and plunging into his beloved New River.[33]

Mrs. Stranahan also devoted her time and energies in support of the Seminole people, and she was instrumental in establishing the federal reservation at Dania in 1926. The education of Indian children was her top priority; she encouraged them to attend the reservation school and worked to have Tony Tommie accepted into the Fort Lauderdale elementary school in 1915.[34] Although he was fifteen years of age, the Seminole youngster had no trouble getting along with his younger classmates, and he learned to read and write fairly well. His only available letter was written to Frank Stranahan in 1916 with the request "I wont you lone me some money $10.00. . . . I wont buy little alligator (like Mr. Stranahan, Tony hatched and sold baby alligators). . . . I wont get my bicyles an shoh and some school books to, if I don't buy little alligator. I paid you back soon."[35] Tommie became a spokesman for the Seminoles living in the Fort Lauderdale area, although his right to speak with authority was disputed by Seminole headmen in other parts of the state.[36] Mrs. Stranahan sponsored the first group of three Seminole children who left the state to attend a federal boarding school for Indians in North Carolina; in 1945, two of these students became the first Seminoles to receive high school diplomas. As she grew older, Mrs. Stranahan organized the "Friends of the Seminoles" to continue her work, and that group has made great contributions to improving the housing, education, and general welfare of the Seminole people. In

32. Nash, "Survey of the Seminole Indians of Florida," p. 54.
33. Bill McGoun, A Biographic History of Broward County, p. 59.
34. Kersey, "Educating the Seminole Indians of Florida, 1879–1970," p. 25.
35. Letter, Tony Tommie to Frank Stranahan, Oct. 4, 1916. Letter in collection of the author.
36. St. Petersburg Daily News, Feb. 15, 1927, p. 4.

addition, Mrs. Stranahan maintained a voluminous correspondence with state and national officials, and it was her tremendous prestige with these public figures which generally brought decisive action favorable to the Indians of Florida.

Ivy Stranahan received numerous accolades for her humanitarian and civic works and was rightfully considered to be the "First Lady" of Fort Lauderdale. Among her many activities, she served as president of the Woman's Suffrage Association of Florida, helped found the Civic Improvement Association and the Garden Club, and was active in the Seventh Day Adventist Church. As a member of the Audubon Society, Mrs. Stranahan actively fought the plume hunters who poached in the rookeries and once gave information to authorities that led to the seizure of $35,000 worth of illegal plumes. She also served ten years on the city planning and zoning board and established the Stranahan Trust to support the Historical Society of Fort Lauderdale, which she served as a trustee until her death. As the city grew, the Stranahans donated numerous tracts of land for schools and parks but never abandoned their original homestead. Mrs. Stranahan continued to live at her "pioneer house" on the river, often reliving the colorful days of the Indian trade for enthralled visitors, until she passed away in 1971 in her ninetieth year.

4

W. H. "Bill" Brown's Boat Landing

Wᴵʟʟɪᴀᴍ Henry "Bill" Brown was a central figure in the Indian trade on the western side of the Everglades at the turn of the century. Of all the permanent trading posts established on the Florida frontier in the last quarter of the nineteenth century, Brown's "Boat Landing" deep in the Big Cypress was the only one which depended exclusively upon a Seminole clientele. For almost two decades, Brown, along with Capt. George Storter at Everglade, dominated the traffic in pelts, plumes, and hides flowing from the Southwest Florida region.

Bill Brown was born in Bristol, England, in 1855.[1] Orphaned as a youth, he was raised by relatives and ultimately apprenticed aboard a ship laying transatlantic cable. The ambitious youngster decided that he would rather take his chances in the new world, so he jumped ship when it arrived in Havana, Cuba; while the English crew and local authorities searched for him, he hid out in palmetto scrub with the aid of a Negress who supplied him with food and blankets. In the 1870s he made his way to Florida, probably aboard

1. Brown was actually born Joseph Goodhind on Dec. 16, 1855, the son of Joseph and Mary Ann Goodhind of the city and county of Bristol, England. Brown had confided this information to his immediate family but gave no firm reason for changing his name when he reached this country. However, it was not uncommon for immigrants to adopt a surname, particularly those who did not want to be traced for some reason, or who felt an "American" name would be more suitable in the new land. In 1971 an official record of birth, naming the parents, place, and date of birth supplied by Brown before his death, was obtained by his family. *Certified Copy of an Entry of Birth BC 737720*, General Register Office, Somerset House, London, June 17, 1971.

one of the cattle boats that plied the route from Havana to Punta Rassa, which was the marshaling point for the cattle drives originating in the broad prairies of southern Florida. For a while he worked in the cattle camps around Arcadia and lived with the Parker family; he also did some trading with Indians. In 1870 Brown married sixteen-year-old Jane Jernigan of Arcadia; Rosa Lee, the first of their ten children, was born in 1882, followed by Mary in 1884 and Frank in 1886.[2] With a growing family to support, Brown had decided to move to central Lee County, where his wife's uncle, Frank Tippins, was sheriff.

The beginning of Brown's intensive trading with the Seminole Indians came in the late 1880s, when he and his family would take an ox-cart loaded with hardware, cloth, groceries, guns, and ammunition into the Big Cypress. At that time the Indian camps were over forty miles southeast of Fort Myers, and the Browns would be out for weeks at a time traversing the almost impassable terrain and making camp wherever a dry hammock could be found. The family's return from one of these forays as reported in the local newspaper must have been a colorful event: "Mr. Wm. H. Brown came in from the Everglades Tuesday bringing his wife and four children, two wagons, 4 yoke of cattle, 3 dogs, 513 gator hides, seven otter hides, 10 Seminole chickens, 3 pigs, thirty pounds of buckskin and 4 pounds of alligator teeth."[3]

In the early years, Brown worked out of Parker's store in Fort Myers, but he found that a permanent base closer to the Indian camps was needed if the volume of his trading was to increase. The family's first home was in a hammock about seven miles west of "Gopher Ridge." Next they moved to a bay hammock three miles further east and opened a store where Indians came to trade. In 1891 the Women's National Indian Association (WNIA) established a Seminole mission at the old "Allen Place" some forty miles southeast of Fort Myers. The mission station covered half a section of land, had a house, barn, and school, as well as a medical missionary family, Dr. and Mrs. J. E. Brecht, in residence.[4] Furthermore, a U.S. Government station for the Indians was soon established on eighty

2. Brown Family Bible. Information provided by Mr. Percy Brown, Immokalee.

3. *Fort Myers Press*, Dec. 10, 1891, p. 8.

4. U.S., Congress, House, *Report of the Commissioner of Indian Affairs,* Exec. Doc. 1, 53d Cong., 2d sess., 1893, p. 356.

acres adjacent to the mission. By then the Brown family had already established a homestead and was instrumental in naming the new community. When the Episcopal Church took over the mission in 1893, Bishop William Crane Gray asked young Rose Brown—who was the first white child confirmed in the region—what the Indian name for "my home" would be, and she told him "I-mok-a-li."[5] The Bishop, in applying for a post office at the mission, converted this to the phonetic Immokalee, and the town has retained that name to the present day. The Brown children attended the school at the mission and were part of a bizarre incident in which the teacher gave the white children Indian names in order to qualify for the additional subsidy which the WNIA provided for Indian children in attendance; Rose Brown Kennon recalls that she was listed as "Tom Billie" on the class role.[6] This subterfuge was soon discovered by a school inspector from Lee County, which withdrew its support from the venture. Since there were too few white children and absolutely no Indians to support a school, the Brown children received a rudimentary education at home from their mother.

Despite the best efforts of Dr. Brecht, who had become the U.S. Indian agent, the government station failed to induce the Seminoles to learn vocational pursuits or receive formal schooling. The Indians would come and visit with the Brechts, perhaps receive some medical aid and stay to eat, inspect the sawmill and other facilities, then return to their wilderness. Nor did the Episcopal missionaries sent out by Bishop Gray, the Rev. and Mrs. H. O. Gibbs, have any success in gaining converts. The Indians loved to listen to the music during the services at Christ Church, and many were present for the annual Christmas and Easter celebrations, but tribal customs and religious prohibitions were too strong for Christianity to make any inroads until well after the turn of the century. In addition, the Indians had moved their camps even further into the Big Cypress with the coming of settlers to the Immokalee area. After a few years, Bill Brown again decided to move closer to the Indian hunting grounds if he could find a suitable site to build a permanent facility.

5. "Address of the Bishop," *Journal of the Second Annual Convocation of the Church in the Missionary Jurisdiction of Southern Florida* (Key West, 1894), p. 49. The story of the naming of Immokalee was also confirmed in a taped interview with Mrs. Rose Brown Kennon, Fort Myers, Sept. 24, 1971. Tape and transcript in University of Florida Indian Oral History Archives, Florida State Museum, Gainesville.
6. Interview with Mrs. Rose Brown Kennon.

This meant taking his family into the wild country on the very edge of the sawgrass of the Everglades.

In 1896 Brown established a store in the Big Cypress. Five years later he bought out J. A. Wilson, a trader and part time Baptist preacher, who had settled about thirty miles southeast of Immokalee. An acre of land was cleared for a house, store, barn, and various outbuildings. A shallow canal was dug out some hundred yards to the deep water so that the Seminoles could pole their dugout canoes right up to the front steps of the store at the "Boat Landing." This was the perfect location from which to reap the bounty of the vast, watery hunting grounds which were the Everglades before the drainage programs had begun. The "Boat Landing" was strategically located at the head of canoe navigation on the western edge of the sawgrass; formerly the Indians hunting in the upper reaches of the Big Cypress had to pole to Miami, three days away, to Stranahan's store at Fort Lauderdale in the same amount of time, or down to Storter's at Everglade, which took four days. With the coming of Brown to the water's edge, the hunters had an alternate market for their products. Now they could work the whole width and breadth of the Everglades country south of Lake Okeechobee and never be much more than a day or two away from a buyer and source of supplies. The volume of alligator hides, otter and raccoon skins, as well as egret and other plumes coming through the "Boat Landing" prior to 1908 was high, and these were prosperous years for Brown.

Some idea of the nature and extent of Brown's business can be obtained from listings carried in regional newspapers, primarily the weekly *Fort Myers Press*. Regular reports of his trading activities began to appear in 1901, the April 18 edition of the *Press* noting that "Mr. W. H. Brown was in town this week from the Indian camps, and informs us that he has bought out J. A. Wilson's store in the Everglades. 'Bill' is the oldest Indian trader in the country and has the confidence of the Seminoles in his dealings with them." The following June 27 it was reported that "Mr. W. H. Brown was in town from his store in the Everglades last Tuesday bringing in 220 gator hides which he disposed of to R. A. Henderson." This was followed by a July 25 entry that "Mr. W. H. Brown and his son were in from their Big Cypress store on Monday, bringing in 525 gator hides and carrying out a load of merchandise to supply the Indians." In 1904 there were three interesting entries concerning the activities at the "Boat Landing." A June 16 edition reported that Brown had brought in "247 gator hides, feet, etc.," while on October 27 he was reported as "bringing in 400 gator hides." With a change in season the Indians turned to trapping for fur, and on December 29 the *Press* reported that "Bill Brown came in from the Big Cypress on Tuesday, bringing 180 otter skins, the biggest catch of the season. The skins represented a money value of nearly one thousand dollars." However, the prime years were 1905 and 1906, and the entries tell their own story. The October 12, 1905 paper headlined "Thirteen Hundred Gators Less in the Everglades" over the following entry: "Bill Brown's big ox wagons came in from the Big Cypress store on Tuesday, bringing in 1270 gator hides, the largest number ever bought here at one time. It is only 3 weeks ago since 'Bill' brought in a shipment of over 800 hides. 'Bill' says he is doing his best to get all the gators in the Everglades before Gov. Broward carries out his drainage schemes. Bill sold his hides to R. A. Henderson, receiving a little over $1,000 for this three weeks haul of hides." A similar bounty was reported on February 8, 1906 under the heading "A Fine Otter Hide," with the story "Bill Brown arrived from the Everglades, Monday, with a big load, including 172 otter hides, 250 gator hides, 75 round skin gator hides, 160 gator feet and some coon skins. One of the otter hides was the largest ever seen here from a Florida otter and measured 5 feet 10 inches in width across the double hide. Ordinary otter hides are worth about $8.00 and a fine one like this will probably bring $12.00 to $15.00." These entries in the *Press* confirm many of the estimates of quantity and prices of alligator and otter hides offered by surviving members of the Brown family.

The mechanics of trading at the "Boat Landing" were similar to those at most of the other frontier posts. When the Indians brought their goods to the store, Brown and his older children, who had learned the Mikasuki language spoken by the Seminoles living in the Big Cypress, waited on them individually. Alligator hides were measured on a long board marked off in feet, and the going price was generally ten cents a foot up to eight feet; later a sliding scale was developed of fifty cents for a five-foot 'gator, seventy-five cents for a six-footer, and a maximum of ninety cents for eight feet or more.[7] Thus, it did not behoove the Indians to bring in anything

7. Interview with Mr. W. Frank Brown, Immokalee, Sept. 24, 1971. Tape and transcript in University of Florida Indian Oral History Archives, Florida State Museum, Gainesville.

larger than eight feet or smaller than five feet. This worked as sort of an economic check on overkilling the smaller breeding 'gators; also, there is no report that Brown ever bought baby gators for the tourist trade, probably because of the problems involved in marketing them. In addition to the belly skins, which were the only part of the alligator suitable for tanning, the Indians occasionally skinned out small 'gators, variously called "hornbacks" or "round hides," for use as decoration on handbags, and brought in alligator teeth for use in making necklaces. They also brought in otter skins and some raccoon skins, as well as egret plumes, the latter usually being mounted on crossed sticks. Cured buckskin was bought by the pound. All of these items were taken by ox-cart into Fort Myers and traded, first with H. P. Parker, and after he went out of business, with R. A. Henderson. Rose Brown Kennon recalls unloading her father's cart with the help of Harvey Heitman, Parker's nephew and later a prominent merchant in his own right, and measuring the alligator hides on the big board at Parker's store. The average price which Bill Brown got for an eight-foot 'gator hide ranged between eighty-five cents and $1.25, so his profit margin was not very great.[8] Otter skins of high quality brought in the neighborhood of two to eight dollars, while a raccoon skin was worth only twenty-five to fifty cents depending on the quality and market demand.[9] Evidently the market for all of these items fluctuated greatly from month to month and year to year, and the traders such as Brown were taking a calculated risk in their dealings with the Seminoles.

On their return trips to the "Boat Landing," the ox-carts would be loaded with 355-lb. barrels of sugar, 196-lb. barrels of grits, and sacks of flour which the Browns would sell by the paper bag full to the Indians.[10] Rifles, shotguns, and ammunition of all types were in demand, especially single shot 32s, level action 38s, and 12–16 gauge shotguns; a 32 caliber rifle sold for approximately seven to eight dollars. Canned goods of all types, cloth in three- to ten-yard bolts, skinning knives, farming implements, and hardware items such as pots, pans, and skillets, as well as some harness were also sold. White sewing machines retailed for twenty-five dollars, and both men and women learned to use them.[11] For personal adornment the

8. Interview with Mrs. Rose Brown Kennon.
9. These prices are quoted in Lawrence E. Will, *A Cracker History of Okeechobee*, pp. 91–92.
10. Interview with Mr. W. Frank Brown.
11. Ibid.

Indian women bought great quantities of beads (three dollars a quart) and the men purchased derby hats, watch chains, and vests. All of these items were purchased one at a time, and paid for with the money that had just previously been received for their trade goods. After the trading was concluded, those Seminoles who were good friends of the Brown family would cross the covered porch connecting the store and living quarters, and spend some time visiting Mrs. Brown and the other children. Some would spend the night or several days at the "Boat Landing," especially during the holiday season, when the Browns held their famous barbecues, but most of them returned to their own nearby camps at the end of the trading day.

Life at the isolated trading post was seldom dull, especially for the older Brown children, who spoke the Indian language and spent great amounts of time learning their ways. Frank Brown was particularly close to the Seminole Billy Conapatchee, who had lived several years with the family of Capt. F. A. Hendry of Fort Myers and attended school there with the Hendry children.[12] One of Conapatchee's sons, Josie Billie, was the same age as Frank, and they became life-long friends. Josie Billie became a Chief Medicine Man of his people and, many years later, a convert to Christianity. The young white boy would spend weeks at a time with Billy Conapatchee, his sons, and brothers Miami Billy and Billy Fewell (also known as "Key West Billie" because he once paddled his canoe to that island city)[13] in hunting throughout the Big Cypress. In the process, Frank Brown came to know this aqueous wilderness as no other white man and was a highly sought guide throughout most of his adult years. He recalls that the best time for hunting was during the high-water months of late summer and early fall, although there were some summers when prolonged drought left the Big Cypress so dry that an ox-cart could be driven across most of the countryside without ever getting the axle wet. In such conditions the alligators clustered in the deep water lakes and 'gator holes and were easy pickings for hunters. During one of these periods, a group of Seminoles borrowed one of the Browns' ox-carts and began a sweep toward Everglade, dispatching 'gators with rifle and axes as they found them. After two weeks they delivered approximately

12. Harry A. Kersey, Jr., "Educating the Seminole Indians of Florida, 1879–1970," pp. 19–20.
13. Clay MacCauley, "The Seminole Indians of Florida," p. 485.

seven hundred hides to Capt. G. W. Storter's store, and on the return trip brought the same amount to the "Boat Landing."[14]

Frank Brown, like most of the men and many of the women living on the Southwest Florida frontier, engaged in the plume trade which flourished prior to the federal law of 1900 banning the plume traffic from both domestic and foreign sources. He recalls once getting fifty dollars for a spread of egret plumes which he sold to a visitor at the Royal Palm Hotel in Fort Myers. After the pluming laws were passed, however, he turned to protecting the rookeries and in 1912 served four months as the Audubon warden at one of the newly established plume bird sanctuaries in Monroe County.[15] Later, in 1918, he was hired by U.S. Indian Agent Frank Brandon to be the first resident supervisor on the Big Cypress Federal Indian Reservation.[16] This 42,000-acre preserve included in its boundaries much of the territory which Brown had roamed in his youth, including the old site of the "Boat Landing" which his family had abandoned shortly after the turn of the century. He moved his wife and children into one of the cottages that had formerly been part of an Episcopal mission on the northwest corner of the reservation land, and supervised the construction of the first permanent Bureau of Indian Affairs station for the Seminole Indians in Florida. After several years, Frank Brown left the government service and settled in Immokalee, where he engaged in ranching and farming, as well as continuing to lead hunting parties into the Everglades.

The oldest of the Brown children, Mrs. Rose Brown Kennon of Fort Myers, also retains many memories of life at the "Boat Landing" at the turn of the century. In addition to working in the store with her father and brother, young Rose was in charge of the family's domestic animals and garden. One day she badly injured a finger, and by nightfall the telltale red streaks of blood poisoning had begun to creep up her arm; there seemed little that the family could do short of amputating the arm to save her life. In desperation they sent for the old Seminole medicine man, Doctor Tommie, and he vowed he could save the young girl's hand. After more than seventy years the events of those days are indelibly etched in her memory: "One of the Indians who spoke English said 'Alushee (Rose), Doctor Tommie want to see your hand.' I went over to where he was

14. Interview with Mr. W. Frank Brown.
15. Ibid.
16. Roy Nash, "Survey of the Seminole Indians of Florida," p. 68.

sitting. He had on a long shirt, no pants, a big wide leather belt, and a little shawl twisted around his head. His hair was white. He said 'finger sick ojus?' He would say English words and say Indian with it. I showed him and he said 'Holiwogus' (plenty bad). He told me to get chopee (hatchet) and butcher knife (chuluskee). . . . I went with him and he told me to get a bucket and he got seven or eight little white roots . . . we washed them and went out to the wood pile and he built a little fire . . . it boiled and boiled and the water became a greenish-yellow. . . . He commenced talking to God (E-shock-e-tom-e-see) telling Him that he was boiling the roots for Alushee . . . told me to stick my hand in the bucket two times a day . . . all the skin began to come back on my hand."[17] This was just one of many kindnesses shown the Brown family by the Seminole people, and it was with great sadness that Bill Brown reported the death of Doctor Tommie in 1904.[18]

Jane Jernigan Brown played a quiet but crucial role in supporting her husband and rearing a large family at their "Boat Landing" home. Seven of the Brown children were born during the years that the Seminole trade was at its height: Ruby (1888), Edwin (1891), Carrie (1893), a baby Joseph (1896) who lived less than a year, the twin boys Sampson and Dewey (1898), and Sarah in 1900.[19]

As she reared her own youngsters, Mrs. Brown also opened her home to visiting Indians, particularly the squaws and Seminole children who accompanied their men to the store. She taught them many domestic arts such as using a sewing machine, which both men and women learned, and in turn they taught her how to use many of the products of the Everglades, such as wild lemon, swamp cabbage, and various herbal medicines. From time to time the Indians would come to the Brown home for emergency medical aid for wounds, cuts, or diseases like measles for which their medicine men had no ready cure. While teaching her own youngsters the three R's because they were so far removed from a regular school, Jane Brown also taught several of the Seminole men to write their names and read a little from the primer. After an Episcopal mission had been established a short distance from the "Boat Landing" and a few Indians began to go there occasionally, one of the missionaries noted: "This morning about 10 o'clock I went out on the porch

17. Interview with Mrs. Rose Brown Kennon.
18. *Fort Myers Press*, June 16, 1904, p. 8.
19. Brown Family Bible.

where they were sitting and began reading a Creek tract, entitled 'Chesus oh-a-utes' (come to Jesus), to them. I had stumbled through half a page of it, when Talu surprised me by saying: 'Gim me, I read him, ojus.' So he took the tract and went at it. I was surprised that he even knew the letters, but he did. He was probably one of Mrs. Brown's former pupils."[20]

Because of its great distance from the nearest towns—two days' travel to Immokalee and five to Fort Myers—and the arduous journey by ox-cart, Mrs. Brown and the younger children rarely left the "Boat Landing" during much of the year. Sometimes in the late summer the family would return to their Immokalee homestead to raise a crop of tomatoes, corn, and the like, but most of the time they saw few other whites at their frontier post. However, one regular visitor and a great favorite of the Brown children was Bishop William Crane Gray. A softspoken, kindly man with a flowing beard, Gray had assumed his Episcopate in the Missionary Jurisdiction of Southern Florida in 1893; already fifty-seven years of age, he would spend the next two decades riding circuit in a region that was still essentially a raw frontier. One of the bishop's major concerns was establishing viable mission work among the Seminole Indians; therefore he was quick to accept the offer of the Women's National Indian Association's holdings that were to become Immokalee. From the start, the Browns were close to the bishop. Rose had helped him name the mission and later was the first white child that he confirmed there; and he had often visited in their home at Immokalee, as well as in their temporary camps in the Everglades. After the Brown family moved into the Big Cypress, Bishop Gray decided to follow their lead and move closer to the Indian camps.

In 1898 the Episcopal Church purchased a section of land and located "Everglade Cross" mission on a site three miles northwest of Brown's store. A small cottage was built, called Everglade Lodge, where the missionaries from Immokalee could spend a few months of each year—preferably during the peak trading months when the Seminoles frequented the vicinity. A two-story hospital facility was added after a medical missionary, Dr. W. J. Godden, located there permanently in 1905. Each year the bishop tried to make his annual visits at a time when the missionaries were in residence at "Everglade Cross" in order to maximize his possibility of contact with the Indians. On these visits he would always attempt to see the

20. Harriet Randolph Parkhill, *Mission to the Seminoles*, p. 15.

Browns, and his diary for April 1903 records one of the more pleasant reminiscences of their association: "Tuesday, 28—We slept well in our 'glades cottage' last night, and after an early breakfast drove three miles through water nearly all the way to the 'landing place' where 'Bill Brown' has his store and his family. A number of Indians had just gone out into the glades, but Willie Tigertail and Charley Tiger were still there. Mrs. Brown and daughter gave us an urgent invitation to dinner, which we accepted. The house was small and entirely surrounded by water, a number of Indian canoes being fastened almost at the very door. Had much valuable conversation with Brown and the others, until dinner. After which Frank and Edwin took me in an Indian canoe far out into the Everglades, where we gathered some beautiful lilies and other flowers. I decided to hold service and preach at the store under these novel circumstances. I took the entire service, leaving Rev. Gibbs in the congregation to respond. Our flowers decorated the counters. I raised the tunes and preached to a congregation of fourteen. I told them, I was sent to 'every creature' as much to them as everyone else."[21] Although some Episcopal missionaries generally did not approve of Brown and other white traders in the Big Cypress because they were potential sources of liquor for the Indian, and once those at "Everglade Cross" objected somewhat petulantly that the Browns' barbecue at Christmas had kept the Indians away from their services, the bishop continued his ties with the family and thoroughly trusted Brown's judgment in matters pertaining to the Seminoles.

Bill Brown was the type of man who inspired confidence by the way he met the challenge of life in the Big Cypress region and wrested a livelihood from its waters, hammocks, and Indian inhabitants. A slight man of medium height, he sported thick mustachios and usually wore a colorful neckerchief and a wide-brimmed hat set on the back of his head. He was not given to loud or abrasive language—except when his ox-cart became mired on the track to town—and the ever present trace of an English accent always set him apart from the cracker dialect spoken in the area. The Indians called him "Mackillasee" (foreigner), and by all accounts he was one of the most trusted white men with whom they dealt, ranking along with Capt. F. A. Hendry, Frank Stranahan, and George Storter in their esteem. There are numerous tales of Brown's dealings, both

21. Ibid., p. 7.

economic and social, with the Seminoles, and a few are worth re-
peating to get the flavor of the man.

One of Capt. Storter's sons, who worked in his father's trading
post at Everglade early in this century, recounts that one day he was
helping his father measure an alligator hide that had been brought
in by an Indian new to the area. The Seminole quizzically viewed
the inch and foot marks notched on the measuring board, and finally
asked: "How many inch yard?" Storter of course replied that there
were 36 inches in a yard, and asked why he wanted to know. The
old Indian shook his head slowly and muttered "Ga-damn, Billy
Brown he tellum forty-two inch yard!"[22] Although this tale is un-
doubtedly true, it is inconsistent with Brown's reputation for fair-
ness; furthermore, the Seminoles traded at enough different stores
that they would have soon picked up such a discrepancy since they
were shrewd businessmen and were seldom cheated in their dealings with whites. More than likely, the Indian in question was trying
to get a few cents added to his hide price by complimenting Storter
on his honesty.

Brown was not noted as being an excessive drinker, but, like most
men of the region, he was not above celebrating over a convivial jug
with his friends, be they white or Seminole. After one session at
which the trading and drinking had apparently finished in a dead
heat, the Indians began to dance about the campfire, the long knee-
length shirts that the men wore in those days whirling about them
in a blur of color. Not to be outdone, "Bill" unbuckled his trousers
and joined the dancers clad only in his shirttails! There is no account
of whether Jane Brown was present at the occasion, or of her reaction, if any, to such a soirée.

By 1908 Bill Brown had determined to sell his "Boat Landing"
holdings and return to Immokalee. Two factors entered into this
decision. First, his wife's health had begun to give way under the
strain of life at the trading post; after twelve years she wished to
return to a more congenial community setting where there were a
regular church, neighbors, a doctor, and schools. Her growing concern over the lack of educational opportunities for the youngsters is
apparent from an announcement in the Fort Myers Press that "A
public school has been established at Mr. Brown's which opened
Monday with Miss Pearl Youmans as teacher."[23] This special ar-

22. Anonymous.
23. Fort Myers Press, Jan. 9, 1908, p. 3. When the Brown family returned

rangement with the Lee County School Board was to be short lived, for a month later the *Press* of February 6 announced that "Wm. H. Brown has sold his store at the Everglades to Dr. Godden, and is going to move back to his place here."[24] The second reason for Brown's move was that he had foreseen the beginning of the end of the truly profitable trade in pelts, plumes, and hides as a result of the drainage of the South Florida wetlands which was just getting under way. In any case, he decided to sell out and return to a more stable life style.

Upon learning that Brown planned to leave, Bishop Gray opted to buy the "Boat Landing" as a new site for the Episcopal mission. He reasoned that it was a spot which the Indians were already in the habit of visiting, and that they would continue to do so when it changed hands; if so, this would provide the missionaries closer contact with the Seminoles in pursuing their medical and spiritual work. An even greater motivation may have been to keep the store from falling into the hands of a whiskey seller, probably the well-known "Uncle" Frank Wilkison who reportedly trafficked in liquor, for the bishop mentioned this as part of his reason for the purchase. At the church convocation of 1909, Bishop Gray announced that $1,500 had been paid for the "Boat Landing," and that in the future all mission activities would be centered there.[25] Now, in addition to his medical duties, the patient Dr. Godden was also to become a storekeeper! The bishop had guessed correctly that the Seminoles would continue to frequent the store, and the *Press* periodically reported the appearance of Dr. Godden's ox-cart loaded with 'gator hides and furs in Fort Myers. In 1910, he wrote the editor of the *Palm Branch*, a diocesan newspaper, that "The medical branch of the work is helping to bring the Indians to us. The store also attracts

---

to their home in Immokalee, "Bill" took an active part in school affairs. On Mar. 4, the county school board minutes indicate that "W. H. Brown and M. F. Youmans appeared before the board to show cause why the Immokalee school house should not be moved," while the Oct. 7 minutes record that "returns of the special election held at Immokalee, Saturday, October 3rd, were canvassed. Said returns showed that all votes cast were in favor of the special tax district and a levy of three (3) mills for the next two years. M. F. Youmans, W. H. Brown, and S. B. Platt received the highest number of votes, and are declared the three trustees of the district for the succeeding two years." Lee County School Board, "Minutes, 1908," 303:176, 190.

24. *Fort Myers Press*, Feb. 6, 1908, p. 1.
25. Protestant Episcopal Church, *Fifteenth Annual Report of the Southern Florida Branch of the Women's Auxiliary to the Board of Missions* (Orlando, 1908), p. 5.

many, but it must not be supposed that this is a source of revenue
for the Mission, although so far it has about paid its own way with
a little help."[26] This may have indicated the beginning of a decrease
in the volume of goods being traded by the Seminoles, and certainly
profits would be adversely affected by the soon-to-be-passed anti-
pluming laws.

Like most missionaries, Dr. Godden was anxious to see the Seminoles turned to more domestic pursuits; in the same letter he proposed the development of an instructional farm for the Indians
which would enable them not only to learn better methods of cultivation, but also to prepare for the inevitable time when they could
no longer depend upon hunting and trapping as their major source
of income. "An industrial branch," he wrote, "is much to be desired for the work here. It would have at least a threefold objective,
being first, another bond between the Indians and ourselves, second,
it would help them at the time pecuniarily and assist them in making their living. This they now do by hunting the alligator and otter
and selling their hides, but the hunting season will soon be a thing
of the past, as a means of livelihood."[27] Bishop Gray, who had long
supported the idea of a permanent reservation for the Seminoles and
an economic life based on agricultural pursuits, eagerly embraced
Dr. Godden's suggestions and set about securing financing for the
venture. The "Boat Landing" was abandoned in 1913, and all of the
mission buildings were moved to a 160-acre site that had been
cleared on the western edge of the Episcopal Church's section of
land.[28] The project got off to a good start, but when Dr. Godden
passed away the following year, the "Seminole Farm" had to be
abandoned by the Church; Bishop Gray had retired, and no successor with Dr. Godden's devotion and interest in the Indians could be
found to take his place. W. Stanley Hanson of Fort Myers, a great
friend of Dr. Godden and the Seminole people, was appointed agent
to liquidate the mission holdings; somewhat ironically, Bill Brown

26. *Palm Branch*, April 1910, pp. 2–3.
27. Ibid.
28. It appears that both the "Boat Landing" and "Seminole Farm" sites were
located on Federal land acquired for the Seminoles prior to 1899; thus, in effect,
the Episcopal Church was a "squatter" and had to obtain permission from the
Department of the Interior to continue the mission work on Federal lands.
The details of this arrangement are found in James W. Covington, "The
Florida Seminoles: 1900–1914," paper presented to the Florida Historical
Society, May 11, 1973.

was the major purchaser of the perishable goods and livestock, which he used at his farm and store in Immokalee.

The Brown family continued to farm, raise some cattle, and run a general store in Immokalee, where they were often visited by their Seminole friends, until "Bill" Brown passed away in 1927 in his seventy-second year. Certainly it is one of those not too uncommon coincidences of history that his passing coincided with the end of the great period of Indian trading in Florida.

Raulerson's store at Okeechobee ca. 1906

Meserve's store at Okeechobee ca. 1915

Indians at Stranahan's store with otter hide on a "shingle", ca. 1899.

Seminoles hunting manatees in the New River ca. 1890s

Seminole hunting party on the New River ca. 1904

Stranahan's store at Fort Lauderdale ca. 1897

Seminoles on Miami River with Julia Tuttle home in background ca. 1890s

W. Frank Brown (left), unknown friend (right), hunting in Big Cypress

5

Catering to the Cow Creek Seminoles

IN 1896 Peter Raulerson, with his wife and family, arrived at Taylor Creek—named after Col. Zachary Taylor, who had defeated the Seminoles there in 1837. He had driven three yoke of oxen down from Polk County in search of open range land for his cattle, and he found what he was looking for in "the bend" where the creek took a big eastward swing prior to emptying into Lake Okeechobee. Raulerson fenced this thirty-mile frontage and built a rambling, two-story log home that is still occupied by members of the family. In the early years the Raulerson home became the hub of practically all social activity in the sparsely settled region.

As other settlers began to drift into the vicinity with their children, there was need for a school, and a room of the Raulerson's house was devoted to that purpose. On Sunday afternoons, Mr. Raulerson would go up and down the creek and all the way out to the Kissimmee River, collecting children who would live at his house and attend school during the week; they were delivered home the following Friday. He also paid part of their tuition fees to insure that there would be a school for his own children to attend. The teachers were sent out by Brevard County, in which the settlement was located, and they, too, lived at the Raulerson home. The best-remembered of these teachers was Miss Tantie Huckabee, a vivacious "Dresden doll" redhead from South Carolina, who gave her name to the settlement when a post office was established there in 1902.[1] For years the mail had been haphazardly brought to "the

1. Will, A Cracker History of Okeechobee, p. 128. Also confirmed in an

73

bend" in the saddle bags of cowboys and other visitors, but as the population grew there was need for regular postal service. Mrs. Raulerson was appointed the first postmistress and operated out of a valise kept under one of the beds in her home. It was she who, when seeking a name for the new post office, decided to call it Tantie after her star boarder and friend. Evidently the schoolmarm had no objections to the use of her name, and so the community remained Tantie for the next decade, until it was renamed Okeechobee in 1912. Even so, many old timers in the region continued to call the town Tantie well into this century. When the city was finally incorporated in 1915, it was almost taken for granted that Peter Raulerson would serve as its first mayor.[2]

In 1905, Peter's son, L. M. Raulerson, opened a general store on the bank of Taylor Creek, about 150 yards from his home.[3] Much of the material used in constructing the store had to be brought up the creek by boat. At first the supplies which he sold in the store came by steamboat down the Kissimmee River from the town of Kissimmee, where most were bought at Makinson and Company; they were off-loaded at Bassenger, then brought the eighteen miles overland by ox-wagon on nearly impassable roads. Some supplies were also brought in this way from Fort Pierce. Later, they sent to Fort Myers for supplies, before the railroad came.[4] The hyacinths clogging the creek kept large steamboats from navigating to Raulerson's store but did not impede the shallow-draft canoes of the Seminole Indians who were his steady customers. After the store opened, the post office was transferred from the Raulerson home and remained there until the store was moved to a new location.[5] With the arrival of the Florida East Coast Railroad in 1915, the town of Okeechobee was platted one mile west of Taylor Creek, and a wide, tree-shaded mall connected the new and old sections of the town. Lewis Rauler-

interview with Mr. and Mrs. Ellis Meserve, Okeechobee, July 28, 1972. Tape and transcript in University of Florida Indian Oral History Archives, Florida State Museum, Gainesville.

2. Alfred Hanna and Kathryn A. Hanna, *Lake Okeechobee*, p. 188.

3. Will, *A Cracker History of Okeechobee*, p. 128.

4. Ibid., pp. 128–29. Also confirmed in an interview with Mr. and Mrs. Hiram Raulerson, Okeechobee, July 28, 1972. Tape and transcript in University of Florida Indian Oral History Archives, Florida State Museum, Gainesville.

5. Will, *A Cracker History of Okeechobee*, p. 128. Interview with Mr. and Mrs. Hiram Raulerson revealed that the post office remained in Raulerson's Store until 1917.

son's new store, a wood and tin structure, was built on the site of the present Raulerson store, and became the center of the business district in the booming town.

The Seminole Indians who lived in the vicinity traded with L. M. Raulerson, whose father and family they had known and trusted for many years. One of the surviving Raulerson children recalls that their father had always treated the Indians with great kindness whenever they visited his home. Many times the Indians ate with the family and were always served before the Raulerson children; she remembers that they were particularly fond of sour milk and fried chicken. The Seminole women took great delight in trying on Mrs. Raulerson's clothing and hats but would never reciprocate by letting her wear theirs. Whenever the Indians wanted to stay overnight, they would set up camp on the wide porches of the Raulerson house or in their front yard. Often the Indians would bring gifts of turkey or deer meat when they came, and they were never turned away. Peter Raulerson learned to speak a patois that mixed English and Creek words and could always communicate with the Indians, though he never learned to speak their language fluently. However, this never hampered his relations with the Seminoles, and they transferred their affection to his family. Once when friction threatened over the removal of the bones of a Seminole leader, the Indians came and warned him to send his wife and children out of the area until the trouble passed over. Raulerson complied and sent the younger children to live with relatives in Bassenger, then took an active role in having the bones returned to their burial place. Until his death, Peter Raulerson remained a close friend of the Seminoles, and his sons and grandchildren continued that tradition. This is particularly evident in the volume of business which the Indians brought to their store.

Early in this century there were Seminole camps strung out around the northern shore of Lake Okeechobee from Fish Eating Creek on the west, up to the Kissimmee River, Taylor and Cypress creeks, and as far east as Cow Creek, where Clay MacCauley had first found part of the Muskogee-speaking element in 1880.[6] From these locations the Indians could hunt the marshy country from the shores of the "big water" north to the Blue Cypress Swamp and the headwaters of the St. Johns River, venture into the higher timber

6. Clay MacCauley, "The Seminole Indians of Florida," p. 478.

country to the northwest, or work east and south into Alligator
Swamp (Hal-pat-i-okee), which was known as "Hungry Land" to
the white settlers.[7] Hunting parties occasionally ventured into the
Everglades proper, south of the lake, and Cow Creek Indians were
known to visit in Miami and Fort Lauderdale. This was a range
abounding in wild life, which afforded the Seminoles a substantial
livelihood as they verged on a shift from basic subsistence to a
trading economy.

The most valuable product that the Seminoles brought to trade
with storekeepers from the late 1880s through the first two decades
of this century were the plumes from the American and snowy
egrets, roseate spoonbills, and even great flocks of green and gold
parakeets which were found along the lake. There were extensive
rookeries "at worm cove between Big Bear Beach and Buckhead
Ridge, as well as on Observation Island, and on Little Bear Beach,
Ritta Island, and in a popash hammock up Taylor Creek . . ."[8] where
the birds were hunted to extinction to meet the demands of the millinery trade. The plumage was most brilliant during the mating season of late spring, and the birds were slaughtered by the thousands,
leaving the eggs and young birds as easy prey for crows, vultures,
and other scavengers. In this manner it did not take the white and
Indian plume hunters long to wipe out the rookeries before the
Lacey Law of 1900 placed the plume birds under federal protection.[9] Even so, the plumes were hunted illegally well into the 1920s,
or as long as there was a market where astronomical prices were
offered. Florida enacted a model nongame bird law in 1901 but
made no provision for enforcement, and Audubon wardens proved
ineffective. It was reported that a single egret plume could bring as
much as five to ten dollars in the illicit market, or up to thirty-two
dollars an ounce—roughly the plumes of four birds.[10]

Next to the plume birds, the Indians derived their greatest per
unit income by trading the pelts of otter, which brought from two to
eight dollars apiece. Otters were trapped during the winter season
when their coats were at their longest and glossiest. The skins were
slit from one hind foot to the other, turned inside out, and stretched
on a wooden shingle cut to fit the pelt. Raccoons were so plentiful

7. Will, A Cracker History of Okeechobee, p. 52.
8. Ibid., pp. 94–95.
9. Hanna and Hanna, Lake Okeechobee, p. 340.
10. Ibid., p. 341.

and easy to trap that they were worth only twenty-five to fifty cents around 1900, but this rose to $1.25 by 1915 and doubled or tripled during the 1920s, when there was a great national demand for coats and other items made of their fur.[11] The 'coon was skinned out with the head attached, and the hides were stretched almost square on a frame of pointed sticks or tacked to wooden shingles before being delivered to the trading posts. Wildcat, panther, bear, and other game around the lake were rarely hunted commercially, although the Indians did bring in wild turkey and deer meat as trade items. As long as this game was plentiful and they had relatively unhampered access to the hunting grounds, the Cow Creek Seminoles showed as little inclination to turn toward domestic pursuits as their Mikasuki brothers to the south of Lake Okeechobee. The Indians continued to live in their scattered chickee camps, cultivated a few small garden plots, raised some cattle and hogs, and carried on their hunting and trapping through the first quarter of this century.

Alligators, of course, were hunted throughout the region for their hides, which were used in making fine leather articles. The going price was ten cents a foot around 1900, with the top price for an eight-foot hide still under one dollar as late as 1915. The belly skin of the 'gator was all that the hunter took, the scaly back being of no commercial use; if the hide was skinned out with the feet attached, it might bring twenty-five cents more, but few hunters went to the trouble.[12] Alligator teeth used to make necklaces reportedly brought five dollars a pound.[13] There is no report of the small "hornbacks" or "round skin" 'gators which were skinned out in their entirety. Neither did there seem to be a market in this region for live baby 'gators, which usually brought twenty-five cents each, due to the lack of a thriving tourist trade such as the coastal towns possessed.

In the winter months, great flocks of ducks and wading birds

11. Will, A Cracker History of Okeechobee, p. 92. One of the most unusual trading posts that the Seminoles frequented was Miss Maud Wingfield's "Floating Store," operated in a houseboat on Lake Okeechobee. After World War I she built a two-story building on the dry lake bottom outside the meander line; when the water rose it was often above the floor of the store. The Indians brought skins and hides to trade for groceries and a wide variety of items. Miss Wingfield's store was demolished by the hurricanes of 1926 and 1928.

12. Ibid., p. 93.

13. Hanna and Hanna, Lake Okeechobee, p. 343.

came to feed on the lake and provided an additional source of food and some income for the Indian hunter. The immensity of this waterfowl population can be gauged by the account of a party traveling in the Caloosahatchee River–Lake Okeechobee region in 1892, which reported "curlew in thousands, duck (teal and mallard) snipe ordinary and whistling, any quantity of herons of all descriptions and simply armies of scout-abouts (coots) and a great number of hooper. . . . Had splendid fun shooting curlew this morning. They kept flying right over the boat so we had only to lay low to get as many as we want."[14]

Seminoles brought their pelts and hides to the Raulerson store and were paid primarily in gold and silver coins on delivery; occasionally some credit was extended when hunting had been poor. In the 1920s, the store ledger revealed that such well known Indians as Billy Bowlegs and Charlie Micco had accounts that were open and active.[15] For the most part, however, the Seminole trade was on a cash-and-carry basis. The Indians bought staple food items: grits, coffee, rice, flour, lard, butter, and fresh fruits such as oranges and apples. Corn, pumpkins, and sweet potatoes were grown in the garden plots at most Seminole camps, but citrus was rarely in evidence to visitors. The women also bought great amounts of fabric and other sewing materials, as well as hand-cranked Singer sewing machines from time to time. L. M. Raulerson knew only a few words in the Muskogee language spoken by the Seminoles, but communication was not any great problem; the Indians just pointed to the items that they wanted on the shelves, then nodded and grunted assent when Raulerson reached for it. The Indians always knew the exact price of the items they wanted and had no trouble in making change or counting their money. By the 1930s, the Indians began to buy Stetson cowboy hats, and blue denim work clothes replaced the tradititonal garb for men—a sign that life on the Brighton Reservation (est. 1938) was oriented toward cattle raising and other agricultural pursuits. About the same time, the store established an account with the "Friends of the Seminoles" organization in Fort Lauderdale headed by Mrs. Stranahan, to supply clothing for Seminole children who were being sent away to federal boarding schools for Indians.

14. Pat Dodson, "Cruise of the Minnehaha," pp. 396, 410.
15. Ledger of L. M. Raulerson & Co., 1912–20. Ledger in collection of Florida Atlantic University.

The Seminoles still trade with the Raulerson family in their modern department store in Okeechobee, just as their fathers and grandfathers have done for over sixty years. Only now, instead of pelts and hides, they deal in credit cards and personal checks or cash as any other member of the community. Even so, until recent years the Raulersons occasionally bought a fine pelt, thus keeping alive the family trading tradition.

When the Seminole people had completed their business at the Raulerson store, they often crossed the wide mall to Meserve's Hardware to trade their plumes for guns, ammunition, and ironware items. Ellis Meserve had arrived on the first train into Okeechobee on the morning of January 4th, 1915, following a thirteen-hour trip from his native St. Augustine. He was nineteen years old and in poor health, but he had left a bank job to seek his fortune in the new community which the Florida East Coast Railroad (F.E.C.) planned at the top of Lake Okeechobee. A friend of the Meserve family, J. E. Ingraham, was vice-president of the railroad and head of its Model Land Company which had platted the new town. He had announced that the extension of the F.E.C. tracks into the area was expected to "develop farmlands, to haul timber and turpentine, to aid the cattle industry, and, most important of all, to provide rapid transportation for the catfish industry of the lake."[16] Ingraham also planned to move the F.E.C. repair shops from St. Augustine to the new location, ostensibly because it was half-way between Jacksonville and Miami—a tortured logic at best. With such plans it was natural for Ingraham to suggest that young Meserve should get in on the ground floor by establishing a hardware store in the future boom town. Ingraham passed away shortly after the project was started and the shops remained in St. Augustine, but the town at the end of the tracks began to thrive. A spur line ran from the main track to a warehouse on Taylor Creek, where fresh catches of fish were received, iced in barrels, and sent on their way to northern markets within a matter of hours; this accessibility led to the establishment of new fish companies on the lake and new jobs. Settlers arrived on each train as well as by boat, a weekly newspaper was started, and on June 4, 1915, Okeechobee City was incorporated and embarked on a decade of rowdy frontier prosperity which lasted until the fishing on the lake played out and the general economic decline

16. Hanna and Hanna, *Lake Okeechobee*, p. 189.

following the Florida "land boom" of the 1920s sent it tumbling into the hard times of the depression years.

Ellis Meserve was to play a significant role in this tumultuous era of the town's history, but he recalls that there was very little there to impress a young man when he arrived on that chilly January morning over half a century ago. In fact, if it had not been for the presence of young Faith Raulerson, he might have returned to St. Augustine and given up on the idea of settling at Okeechobee. When the train arrived at the railhead there was nothing in sight except a little cleared land and the woods beyond; after he had helped the train crew get a fire started to warm themselves, Meserve took his bag and walked down to Taylor Creek to take a look around and saw not another living soul. Evidently he stayed too long, for the train left without him, and he was stranded in the middle of nowhere. Returning to the creek, he came across L. M. Raulerson's store, and the owner directed him to the family home where he might secure lodging for the night. In a hammock on the porch Meserve found "the prettiest girl I had ever seen,"[17] and his interest in the place was renewed. The following day he picked out a lot for his future store and caught the train back to St. Augustine, where his father co-signed on a $4,000 note to cover the building and stocking of a hardware store. After he opened his hardware business, Meserve courted Faith Raulerson, and they were married in 1916; their first home was an apartment over the hardware store, and the Meserves recall sitting on their balcony and watching the fishermen and cowboys brawling and shooting on the typically wild Saturday nights in Okeechobee. One morning in January 1928, Faith Meserve overturned a kerosene stove which ignited the frame structure and burned it to the ground. They rebuilt the store just in time to have it flattened by the famous hurricane in October of the same year. After that they moved into their present home and built a one-story stone store at the old location, where Meserve is still doing business.

In the early years, business was slow for the young storekeeper, so Meserve would often drive his truck around to the south side of Lake Okeechobee and work in Clewiston or Moore Haven hauling vegetables to the loading docks until three or four o'clock in the morning. Then he would return for a few hours sleep before open-

17. Interview with Mr. and Mrs. Ellis Meserve, July 28, 1972.

ing his store to the town and Indian trade. When he first started in business, there weren't over six or seven families, numbering perhaps thirty people in all, in the town; his brother-in-law, L. M. Raulerson, would often kid him by asking, "Sonny boy, who you going to sell your hardware to?" and Ellis would answer, "the same people you sell your groceries to," which meant mostly Indians in those days.[18] About 75 per cent of Meserve's business came from the Seminoles in the early years, and he retains many memories of their visits to the store.

The only items that Meserve accepted in trade from the Seminoles were the plumes of egret and curlew, and occasionally the feathers of other plume birds. He generally judged the quality of the plumes by running his hands through the bundles to feel their texture. The Indians received anywhere from seventy-five cents to one dollar for the fine plumes, and they never questioned Meserve's judgment in the matter because of his reputation for fair dealing; it would also not have been worth their time to travel to another merchant in Fort Pierce or elsewhere for a possible difference of a few cents. Actually, the market price on plumes was subject to such fluctuations that the traders took a businessman's risk in handling them at all. Meserve, for example, shipped his plumes by parcel post to a millinery house in New Orleans on consignment and was never sure just what price they would bring. Although the plume trade was illegal after the federal law of 1900, it persisted well into the 1920s because of the demands of fashion; and it was only the change in women's tastes that brought it to an end, not the Audubon Society or the law.

The hardware items which Meserve sold to the Seminoles were paid for in cash and purchased one at a time; this was the same pattern of transaction as reported at the other Florida trading posts of the period. The Indians did not barter their pelts and plumes per se, but were paid for them and then either used the money to buy items that they needed or saved it. Mostly they purchased rifles and shotguns (thirty-five dollars for a 12-gauge), ammunition (forty-five cents a box for black powder shotgun shells), pots, pans, skillets (approximately one dollar each), hammers, nails, farming tools such as hoes and axes, and a whole range of small hardware items. Meserve recalls that they wanted every item wrapped in paper and tied with twine, perhaps because they had use for these items in

18. Ibid.

their camps. Curiously, though, the Indians always brought their bundles of plumes wrapped in newspaper rather than regular wrapping paper, and Meserve still does not know where they came by their supply of old newspapers.[19] Although he never learned to speak other than a few words of the Seminole language, Meserve found little trouble in communicating in a combination of English, Creek, and sign language. Saturday was the big shopping day for the Seminoles, but they were in and out of the store throughout the week if they had plumes to sell or needed to buy supplies for their camps. Because many of the Seminole camps were close to town, the majority being within a twenty-mile radius, entire families often came to Okeechobee on shopping trips. The women and children would sit in a circle on the floor of his store, laughing, talking, eating, and changing wet babies, while the men carried on their business with Meserve. Sometimes there would be a steady flow of Seminoles between the hardware store and Raulerson's grocery, as the shopping day took on a carnival-like atmosphere for the visiting Indians.

Throughout the 1920s and 1930s, the Indian trade remained a dominant factor in the prosperity of Meserve's business, and he made many lasting friendships with Seminole people. Each year he went hunting with Billy Bowlegs III, the well-known Indian elder. He sold Billy one of the first single-barrel, single-shot, shotguns offered in the store, and it is presently in the possession of the DeVane family of Sebring. Meserve always thought it interesting that Billy Bowlegs was never accepted as a leader of the Seminole people, although they respected him as an elder; the old man lived alone in a camp on Indian Prairie that was far removed from the other Seminole camps, and it was only in his later years that Bowlegs received a good deal of attention through the efforts of various local historians. Some of the numerous vignettes of Indian life that Meserve can recall reveal a straightforwardness of the Indian that is humorous in retrospect. One day Meserve met old Naha Tiger riding into town on his horse, with his squaw walking behind. He asked "Naha, why isn't your squaw riding?" and the Seminole replied matter-of-factly, "Squaw no gottum horse."[20] Obviously there was a difference in cultural values between the white man and the Indian.

Faith Raulerson Meserve also has memories of her contacts with

19. Ibid.
20. Ibid.

the Seminoles as a young girl growing up in "the bend" region at the turn of the century. She particularly recalls the great flocks of wading birds that would turn the sky white as they flew out of the rookeries on Taylor Creek in the morning and returned in the afternoon with their wings catching the pink glow of a setting sun. It was her recollection that the man who caused all the furor by removing the skeleton of Captain Tom Tiger claimed to be an agent of the Smithsonian Institution in Washington, D.C. He stayed at her family home and took back all of the Seminole artifacts that the Raulersons had collected up to that time—so many that it took an ox-cart to get them all to Fort Pierce. It was then that she and the other children were sent to visit relatives in Bassenger until the trouble was cleared up. She also remembers the time that Indian missionaries from Oklahoma stayed briefly at the Raulerson home during a respite from their work in the Seminole camps. Like most of the pioneers in that section of Florida, the Seminoles were just a normal part of everyday life to her, and their presence was almost taken for granted. There was never any major friction between the Indians and the townspeople that she could recall, and that rapport has survived to this day.

Meserve also knew and liked Polly Parker, the woman who has sometimes been called the "Evangeline of the Seminoles" because she escaped from one of the ships that was taking her people to the Indian Territory in Oklahoma. After many months she led a small group of followers back from the Panhandle region of Florida to her home near the Kissimmee River, and the location was named "Polly Parker's Camp" by whites; this was one of the first pieces of land that the "Friends of the Florida Seminoles," headed by Minnie Moore-Willson and Bishop William Crane Gray, tried to purchase as a Seminole reservation early in this century.[21] Polly reportedly had over two hundred descendents in the Seminole tribe, and at her death in 1921 she was buried in a traditional log-pen grave between Okeechobee and what is today the Brighton Reservation. Meserve always enjoyed the old woman's presence in the store, and even though she spoke no English, she was always smiling and nodding to him; today a finely retouched picture of the lady whom the townspeople called "Aunt Polly" hangs in Meserve's Hardware, along with

21. Minnie Moore-Willson, *The Seminoles of Florida*, pp. 68–70. See also Letter, P. A. Vans Agnew to J. M. Willson, June 29, 1926, in collection of the University of Miami.

other Indian pictures, as a tribute to his long association with the Seminole people.

The Cow Creek Seminoles also had permanent camps on the east side of Lake Okeechobee, in the high woodlands between the lake and the swamps that lay before the coastal ridge. Settlers began moving into the area during the 1890s and gave the settlement the name of Indiantown. One of the earliest arrivals was Joe Bowers, a native of South Carolina who had ventured to Florida at age sixteen and settled at Bartow in Polk County.[22] He was soon joined by his brothers, one of whom reportedly rode Joe's favorite horse down from their old home, and they jointly developed various business interests. Later the Bowers brothers sold their Bartow holdings, perhaps as a result of the disastrous freeze of 1894–95, and moved to the Indiantown area, where they bought a large tract of land for citrus and cattle. Dessie Bowers took charge of planting the citrus groves that are still in existence today, while Joe was in charge of developing their cattle herd. A third brother, Frank, moved to the town of Jupiter on the coast and established a general store.[23] All of these enterprises were apparently successful, and the Bowers brothers amassed substantial wealth.

Joe Bowers was a bachelor who spent most of his adult life in the outdoors working cattle, hunting, trapping, and trading, as well as living with the Indians. His only home was a Seminole-style chickee camp, and there he established a small trading post where his Indian friends could bring their skins and hides when in the vicinity. There are no records of the volume and extent of this trading activity, but more than likely Bowers did it more as a matter of convenience than as a profit-making enterprise. The raw goods that he took in trade were shipped and sold through his brother's store in Jupiter, some twenty miles to the east.

Over the years, old Joe Bowers became very close to the Seminoles and was reportedly adopted into the tribe. As a tribute to their friend, many of the Indians opted to use Bowers as their English surname. It is possible that he played a role in calming the Cow Creek Indians during the 1907 incident when the bones of Captain Tom Tiger were removed from their burial place.[24] The tense situ-

22. Hanna and Hanna, *Lake Okeechobee*, p. 232.

23. Interview with Mrs. Ruby Bowers McGehee, Jupiter, Nov. 15, 1972. Tape and transcript in University of Florida Indian Oral History Archives, Florida State Museum, Gainesville.

24. Interview with Mr. and Mrs. Ellis Meserve.

ation was resolved when the bones were returned to the Seminole people and charges were placed against the northern tourist park operator who had caused the uproar; however, he was never brought to trial.[25] The Bowers brothers were also instrumental in bringing the first Seminole Baptist missionaries from Oklahoma in 1907, and may have accompanied the Reverend W. J. Brown when he "preached the first sermon some 22 miles south of Jupiter" that year.[26] Four years later, George Washington, a Seminole missionary from Wewoka, Oklahoma, established a mission station at Bowers Grove. This was the beginning of more or less continuous Baptist involvement among the Seminoles, although the establishment of churches would not come until the 1930s.

In 1911 the U.S. Government purchased a 2,200-acre tract of land near Indiantown in Palm Beach County, now Martin County, as a preserve for Seminole Indians. Many of the Cow Creek families already had permanent camps on the land and remained there until Indian Agent Capt. L. A. Spencer compelled them to move to the Dania Reservation in 1927. Ostensibly, this action was to bring them closer to medical and educational facilities at the newly opened government station there; however, some Indians, such as the Tiger and Gopher families, balked at moving, and Spencer cut their food rations until they capitulated. This tract was traded to the State of Florida in the 1930s in exchange for an equal amount of land adjacent to the existing federal reservations in Glades and Hendry counties.

As Bowers was approaching seventy years of age, he fell in love with a young, blonde girl from Okeechobee who was only twenty years old.[27] They were married in a colorful ceremony attended by some five hundred guests, including many Indians. The bride and groom exchanged vows while on horseback, and the minister was similarly, if somewhat precariously, mounted. Old Joe built his bride a fine house in the citrus grove and moved his somewhat attenuated trading activities there in the 1930s. Apparently the marriage lasted

25. The incident of Captain Tom Tiger's bones is treated in Moore-Willson, *The Seminoles of Florida*, pp. 151–54. Also M. R. Harrington, "Reminiscences of an Archeologist: V," pp. 29–34. However, the most complete contemporary account of the incident is found in the *St. Lucie County Tribune*, Mar. 8, 15, Apr. 12, 19, July 26, 1907.

26. First Seminole Baptist Church, *Dedication Brochure*, 1949, p. 5.

27. Interview with Mrs. Ruby Bowers McGehee. This incident is also reported in Hanna and Hanna, *Lake Okeechobee*, p. 233.

only long enough for the young lady to insure her future financial security at the expense of the usually wily old septuagenarian, so he spent his remaining years among his citrus and cattle, visiting with his Seminole friends. Joe Bowers died in 1945 at the age of seventy-six, and with him passed one of the closest old friends of the Cow Creek Seminoles.

6

The Indian River Traders

O NE MORNING in the first quarter of this century, a youngster hunting in the wilderness west of Stuart encountered a scene that was to remain with him into his mature years when it was reported in a book of reminiscences. "The early rays of the sun were painting golden yellow the trunks of the giant yellow pines across the way. The slough with its borders of saw grass, its margins of bayheads, was still as polished black glass. Then, of a sudden, exploding into the water on the far side, came a pack of dogs of all descriptions— big dogs, little dogs, hounds, mongrels, hog-catchers—all swimming our way. Bursting behind them came a dozen ponies ridden by brown-naked Indian boys, laughing and yelling. Next, sloshing through the water on horseback, came the bucks in their rainbow shirts with rifles and shotguns, and then the little gypsy caravan wagons carrying the squaws, old men and women—and, of course, the furs they were bringing in to 'Kitchee'."[1]

The destination of this trading party was the Stuart store owned by Capt. Walter Kitching, "Kitchee" to the Seminoles, the most prominent early merchant and Indian trader in the lower Indian River country. A native of Leeds, England, he had immigrated to the United States in 1867 at the age of twenty-one; soon after arriving he hired on as a wagon driver hauling supplies to Indians on the western frontier and spent the next fifteen years in that section of the country. Among his other activities, Kitching briefly taught school for Indian youngsters, and because he could not pronounce their native names, followed the white man's custom of assigning

1. Ernest Lyons, *My Florida,* p. 26.

them all anglicized names such as Mary, John, etc. After leaving the Indian school, Kitching entered business and prospered sufficiently that he had investment capital when he came to southern Florida in 1883; he purchased sixteen parcels of land at $1.25 per acre, and began a farming operation.

In 1887 he entered into partnership with a Mr. Travis of Cocoa to establish a "floating store" business along the lower east coast. As captain of the schooner *Merchant* which ran from Cocoa to Jupiter, usually taking thirty days for the trip if the weather was good, Kitching became one of the best known men in the region. Often he would send postcards ahead to settlers along the coast, notifying them of the dates when he expected to make landfall at their settlements, and when the schooner entered the harbors, Kitching had his mate blow a loud blast on a conch shell horn to bring the residents and their children flocking to the docks. He generally sold dry goods, foodstuffs, and medicines to the settlers, gave candy to the children, and also served as Justice of the Peace to perform marriages. On one of these trips Kitching stopped at the home of John Michael in Wabasso, where he saw the picture of Michael's sister Emma, who was soon to visit from Maryland. It was love at first sight. The comely Emma Michael proved to be all that Kitching desired as a wife, and evidently the young lady found the attraction to be mutual, for they were married in 1894.

That same year, Kitching built a home on riverfront property in Stuart, then called Pottsdam, where the family still resides. Two years earlier, Kitching had planted a pineapple field on his land, and his brother, Broster Kitching, came over from England to supervise the operation. In good years the crop would bring as much as ten thousand dollars to the family coffers. When Henry M. Flagler decided to extend his Florida East Coast Railroad south toward Palm Beach, it was Kitching who persuaded him to route the main line through the community by offering both right-of-way and $200 in cash. Flagler declined the cash offer but took the right-of-way, and rerouted the line through the settlement rather than farther inland. In 1894 the track arrived at the town of Pottsdam, but Mrs. Kitching was perturbed that the conductor always called it "damn pots." It was soon renamed for Jack Stuart, who ran a drink stand on the river; settlers would say "let's go down to Stuart's and get a cold drink," so the name stuck.

With the arrival of the railroad at Miami in 1896, the lucrative period of coastal trading by schooners such as the *Merchant* came to an end. Now most goods could be shipped quickly and inexpensively via railroad to the storekeepers in settlements up and down the Florida coast, although there would still be a great volume of bulk shipping by coastal schooners and steamboats well into this century. Seeing this economic change, Kitching decided to settle into the life of a local merchant and sold his schooner in 1897. The year before he had built the first large store in Stuart, a two-story building which featured furniture upstairs, with the main floor divided into dry goods, hardware, and grocery sections. In an attached shed, stock feed and fertilizers were sold to local agricultural interests. From the very outset, Seminole Indians formed a significant portion of the trade at the store, and Kitching's daughter Josephine (Mrs. J. E. Taylor), has some graphic impression of those days:

"My father Walter Kitching had many interesting experiences with the Seminole Indians. Also did my husband John E. Taylor after he came to Stuart, Florida from Oklahoma, and was with Walter Kitching in his General Merchandise Store which he later bought when Father retired. The Indians were quite a tourist attraction as well as a lucrative business.

"Our Mercantile Store was their headquarters. They came to town about two maybe three times a year in their covered wagons. Their path to come was called the Stuart Annie road, now called Rd. 76, Kamer Highway in 1972. They came from the Indiantown area. They spent several days at a time behind our store on the riverside, as Stuart was used as an outlet for the sale of their Otter, Alligator and Coon hides. Most of which were shipped to St. Louis, Mo. The Indians received $7.00 to $8.00 for an Otter hide, with $3.00 to $5.00 according to size for the Alligator, the average Coon hide was $1.00 a piece.

"The Indians received as much as $1,000.00 or more each trip to town. If they had more cash than they wished to carry my Father W. K. was their banker, and he kept it in his money safe in the store until needed again. The Seminoles called my father 'Kitchee!'

"The Indians when trading *always wanted* their money in *gold* or *silver,* not paper money. Each Indian big and little had his own money. When trading in the Store one would buy some dress goods and pay for it, and get the change, then maybe a sack of flour and pay, get the correct silver and so on. This was the only way they could keep track of their money.

"The Seminoles at that time 1897 to around 1916 were very friendly, honest, and with high morals."[2]

Like most of the trading families who dealt with the Seminoles around the turn of the century, the Kitchings had numerous encounters with the Indians that are interesting in the retelling almost three-quarters of a century later. Josephine Kitching Taylor remembers that "as a baby I . . . was sitting on the floor in the dining room one day and my mother Emma Kitching was in the kitchen. On hearing me whimper she turned to see what was wrong with me, and collided with a fat Indian squaw. Mother was so surprised that she screamed. Indians can sneak up so easily in their bare feet. On completing her errand the squaw left, and as far as mother could see she was still shaking with laughter. My father had sent the squaw up to our house to get some extra feed, I think, as he was maybe out of it at the store."[3] There was another instance when "after turning out our lights before retiring one night, we saw an *Indian Buck* peeping in the window. Father Walter Kitching asked him what he wanted? The Indian answered: 'Kitchee buy venison?' Father ended up at the small end of the bargain. He bought some venison, then *gave* the Indian Buck his *saw-knife,* a combination cutter and saw, which fascinated the Seminole."[4] Sometimes the genial Indians, who felt free to enter the Kitching house at will, provided moments of comic relief to the dull routine of life around the store. "One day father and mother were having a carpenter do some repair work in the upstairs bathroom, and on turning around saw a big Indian chief standing at the top of the stairs. He said 'Howdy Kitchee, this your squaw, your papoose?' pointing to mother and me."[5] The Kitching daughter also remembers that one of the best known Indian customers was "Billy Bolec 'Bowlegs' . . . He lived on the Brighton Indian Reservation near the town of Okeechobee, Florida, and belonged to the 'Snake Clan.' He always traded with my father W. K. and husband John Edwin Taylor. John, years later, had his picture taken with 'Billy Bowlegs' on Sunday, Oct. 22,

2. Manuscript prepared for the author by Mrs. John E. Taylor, Sr., of Stuart, Fla., December 13, 1972. Also, a taped interview with Mrs. Taylor on the same date. Tape and transcript in University of Florida Indian Oral History Archives, Florida State Museum, Gainesville. Mrs. Taylor was the only child of Capt. Walter Kitching.
3. Taylor Manuscript.
4. Ibid.
5. Ibid. This is the only reference to the Seminoles calling a child a "papoose" that the author has ever encountered.

1961, not long before he died at 101 years in 1964. When I was a small child 'Billy Bowlegs' *gave me a dime.* I was very pleased and will always remember the nice Seminole Indian Chief."[6]

Not all white pioneers of the Stuart area recall the Seminoles so fondly, perhaps because they did not have such intimate contact with them. A more typical reaction might be that of Ernest Lyons, later editor of the local newspaper, who wrote, "We saw a good many Seminoles in Stuart's early days. But they never did strike me as being happy. They would come into town to trade 'coon hides and otter pelts for staples at Uncle Walter Kitching's big store. The bucks did all the trading, although the squaws indicated what they wanted. When they bought, it was one item at a time. There was always a gulf. It was apparent that they did not trust the white man, not even their good friend 'Kitchee' or his son-in-law John Taylor. Part way, yes, but not far."[7] This account does not appear to take into account the Indians' willingness to let Kitching act as their banker, or the rapport which the trading families established through sheer proximity. In fact, the thinly veiled hostility which the townspeople must have held for the Seminoles is apparent in parts of the Lyons account. "The squaws and pickaninnies—that's what the early residents called the children—would go house to house selling blueberries for ten cents a basket. The trade wasn't very smart because some folks started the rumor that they really weren't blueberries but pokeberries which could poison you. That wasn't true, but it showed the mutual distrust."[8] There was also evidently some friction between Indians and local citizens over hunting rights, for "along about the beginning of hunting season in the fall, the word would circulate that the Indians were coming in to kill all the deer and turkeys and grab off all the 'coons and otter in the backwoods before the white folks could get them."[9]

The pioneer editor's frank, if unflattering, description of the Indians who came to Stuart during his boyhood offers the picture of a people who were far removed from the romantic concept of the Rousseauean noble savage: "All the Indians I had even seen were

6. Ibid.
7. Lyons, *My Florida,* p. 23.
8. Ibid., pp. 23–25.
9. Ibid., p. 25. In a conversation with the author, Lyons confided that a good deal of this animosity stemmed from the Seminole practice of burning off the countryside during hunting season, thereby endangering agricultural interests, as well as disturbing white hunters in the area.

glum, morose and distrustful. The women were loaded with rainbow dresses and petticoats that swept the ground, strings of turquoise beads up to their chins, and they all looked like they needed a bath. They were barefooted. The men wore rainbow shirts down to their knees, sort of like Greek kilts, their legs were scarred and their bare feet as calloused as an alligator's back leather."[10] Lyons confided that he had never reflected on the idea that Indians were not naturally glum creatures, and that perhaps the white man's treatment of them had something to do with their disposition when they were in town, until he saw them in the happy caravan described at the outset of this account. It can only be suspected that he represented the more humane and perceptive element of pioneer Florida society, and that to most townspeople the Seminoles were a matter of no concern whatsoever.

In 1912 the young J. E. Taylor came to Stuart, went to work for Walter Kitching in his store, and later became the cashier at his bank, which was the first one opened in the community. Taylor was a native of Oklahoma, then the Indian Territory, where he had gone to school and associated with Cherokee Indians all his life; thus, he was well suited to deal with the Indian clients at the store. Often he would take a handful of gold and silver coins, shifting them from hand to hand to entice the Indians to come in and trade; the Seminoles generally laughed and accepted his invitation. His dealings with Indians were mild, however, compared to the violence at the Bank of Stuart where he was working in 1915, when it was robbed by the infamous Ashley gang which terrorized the lower east coast of Florida for over a decade.[11]

John E. Taylor married Josephine Kitching in 1914, the same year that Kitching opened a second store. When his father-in-law retired in 1919, Taylor bought out the business and continued to run it for another four years. The young businessman became a prominent figure in civic affairs, serving on the town council and city commission for twelve years, and as mayor from 1920–28. He was also instrumental in having Martin County created by an act of the state legislature in 1925, and was elected as the first state representative from the new constituency. During the Florida "land boom" of the 1920s, Taylor opened the short-lived Seminole Bank of Stuart, which used a likeness of Billy Bowlegs on its checks. Some time before, the

10. Ibid.
11. Hix G. Stuart, *The Notorious Ashley Gang*, pp. 13–15.

Indian trade had come to an end, as described by his wife: "About 1916 the majority of our Indians, Seminoles, stopped coming to trade and sell their wild animal hides. The State of Florida had enacted wild game laws forbidding the killing of alligators and fur-bearing animals. Also, the state had started helping the Indians to make a living."[12]

Although the Kitching family probably was unaware of it at the time, they were witnessing the beginning of the final stage in the evolution of the Seminoles from a subsistence economy, to dependence on traders to market the products of their hunting and trapping, and ultimately to large-scale commercial agriculture on reservation lands. By the 1920s the drainage of the lands around the big lake, increasing agricultural expansion, and a population growth resulting from the "boom," had forced the Seminoles onto farms as workers or into isolated camps where they eked out a marginal existence in a land almost devoid of game. It would not be until the establishment of the Brighton Reservation in 1938, six years after Walter Kitching's death at the age of eighty-six, that his Indian friends would find a permanent home and land to call their own.

At Jupiter, some thirty miles south of Stuart, the meandering Loxahatchee River forms an inlet from the Atlantic. The government had erected a lighthouse at this point in 1860, and the Seminole Indians were accustomed to come there to trade with the families tending the light and to share in the salvaging of goods washed ashore from wrecks at sea. The treacherous tidal currents in the area of the inlet often spelled disaster for unwary captains plying the coastwise trade route between Jacksonville and Key West. One such instance of Seminole involvement in salvage operations was described by C. W. Pierce in his reminiscences, *Pioneer Life in Southeast Florida*:

> The wrecked steamer's name was the *Victor,* one of the Mallory Line from New York, bound for New Orleans. . . . When the shipwrecked people walked up to the house from the dock, they were closely followed by the whole crowd of Indians; each Indian appeared to have his entire family with him, for about half were squaws and there were many piccaninnies, as the Seminoles call their children. They never used the word papoose, and it is very doubtful if they knew what it meant.

12. Taylor Manuscript.

The Indians remained for about an hour, but then, all of a sudden, they started for their canoes, the squaws and piccaninnies trailing along behind. They went up Lake Worth Creek for a short distance and made camp, prepared to stay until there was nothing more to be picked from the wreck. . . . The next day, as the tide started in, the old ship commenced to break up . . . The tide was coming in on a full flood and the water was full of wreckage that had washed in through the inlet. . . . [Pierce's father] saw two Indians trying to get a large container into their canoe. He sculled up alongside and told them it belonged to him; they gave it up without protest or hesitation as there were too many other things floating in the river to waste any time disputing the ownership of any one particular box. In telling of the incident later, father said he knew as soon as he came near that it was a sewing machine and that the Indians would not know what to do with it if he let them keep it [this was the 1870s, and traders had not yet begun to use machines as trade goods]. As he had suspected, it was a Wheeler and Wilson machine and mother used it for many years. . . . When the Indians arrived at Jupiter they were dressed in regular Seminole style with fancy colored shirts that reached to their knees. Some of them also wore brown tanned buckskin leggins and large turbans made from red and black checked shawls that they folded and wound around their heads to form a flat top and bottom. Within a week or so after the breaking up of the Victor, they came to the lighthouse decked out in white shirts and vests. As the white man's shirt was not nearly as long as the regular Indian shirt their new dress left quite a length of bare leg showing.[13]

One of the best-known traders at Jupiter was Ben Hill Doster, who moved his family there in 1894. He came to take over the homestead and store of his sister, Mrs. Gus Miller, whose husband had recently passed away. After surviving the "big freeze" of their first winter in Florida, Doster established a thriving business with the "cracker" hunters, trappers, and fishermen who made their livelihood along the river. Among his customers were also Seminole Indians. A daughter recalled that "They traded hides, plumes, venison for whatever they needed in the stores, and often got soggily drunk at 'blind tigers' operated by designing white men, whose

13. Charles W. Pierce, *Pioneer Life in Southeast Florida*, ed. Donald W. Curl, pp. 34–37.

pasts no one thought of inquiring into, who existed by trickery, thievery, and who often got the Indians drunk in order to cheat them. Once the Indians became thoroughly convinced of this deception, they began to come into Papa's store, who always treated them fairly and gave them full measure of goods for goods. Papa said the finest compliment he ever received was one day when the Indian chief, Tommy Tiger, put his hand on Papa's shoulder and said 'You good man.'"[14] Like most pioneer families in the region, the Dosters had many personal encounters with the Indians that are worthy of retelling. One time the Indians made camp on their property and the family was afraid to leave the house all day until their father returned. Mrs. Doster apparently thought the Indians would assume that no one was at home if she and the children did not stir abroad. That evening as Doster passed on his way home, a Seminole nodded toward the house and commented, "Humph, white squaw scared." Later, the family became accustomed to having the Indians around to the extent of even helping them sober up after drinking bouts.

After a year on the homestead, the Dosters moved into downtown Jupiter, and the family continued to operate the store built on pilings over the river. Doster later built a second store beside the tracks of the Florida East Coast Railroad in the town of West Jupiter and took a younger partner. Freight was brought over from West Jupiter on the family's boat the *Bacon Box* to the Jupiter store. Once in a hurricane the store was blown off its foundations but was later rebuilt. Doster sold his Jupiter holdings around the turn of the century and moved to West Palm Beach.

Near the turn of the century, Frank Bowers, one of the three South Carolina brothers who had originally settled in the Indiantown area, moved his family to Jupiter and established a general merchandise store and trading post on the riverfront. By 1908 he had been appointed postmaster and ran a post office in the store. Ruby Bowers McGehee, the oldest of Frank's two girls and the only surviving member of the clan, retains many memories of her father's transactions with the Indians who came to the store; she also has fond recollections of her colorful bachelor uncles, Dessie and Joe Bowers, who ran the family cattle and citrus interests. They lived Indian-style in a "chickee" and kept a huge black snake as a pet "to keep the rats down" around their place. Joe ran a small store

14. Dora Doster Utz, "Life on the Loxahatchee," p. 40.

where he traded food, calico, beads, and other goods to the Indians, taking otter, 'coon, and other hides in exchange. When he had a load of furs collected or needed supplies from Frank's store, "Uncle Joe" would make the twenty-five mile trip in from Indiantown by mule-drawn wagon (earlier by ox-cart); the trip took him two days with an overnight stop at a small lake so he could feed the fish. Joe Bowers never learned to drive a car, and he rode horseback until the time of his death.[15]

The hides that were brought to Bowers' store in Jupiter were rolled and stacked to the ten-foot ceiling of a storeroom; the otter pelts were always turned inside out to protect the valuable fur. The Bowers' daughter does not recall ever seeing an alligator hide at the store, although she was really not old enough to work in the business. The furs were shipped out by boat from the store dock, and later by railroad.

Seminoles occasionally came in to Jupiter and brought their furs to trade at the store. Most often they purchased food items, calico cloth, beads, candy, and ammunition—but no whiskey, since all of the Bowers brothers were teetotalers. Nevertheless, the Indians could always find liquor on their visits to town. Once an inebriated brave performed an impromptu war dance on the display cases at the store, much to the delight of the Bowers children and the consternation of their father.[16]

In 1927, Frank Bowers had his store jacked off its foundations, placed on a barge, floated down the river, and relocated on a piece of ground in the center of the present-day town of Jupiter. A separate building was erected for the post office. Later, the old store was replaced with a two-story building that is still standing. When Frank Bowers retired from the business in the 1940s, his daughter and son-in-law continued it a while longer. Frank Bowers passed away in Jupiter.

Fort Pierce was established as a military outpost on the Indian River during the Second Seminole War (1835–42) and was named for Gen. Benjamin K. Pierce, whose brother was later to become the fourteenth president of the United States. The early settlers in the region came under the terms of the Armed Occupation Act of 1842,

15. Interview with Mrs. Ruby Bowers McGehee, Jupiter, November 15, 1972. Tape and transcript in University of Florida Indian Oral History Archives, Florida State Museum, Gainesville.
16. Ibid.

which offered each family 160 acres of land if they would settle on the property for five years and hold the territory against the Seminole Indians.[17] This act provided an opportunity for many families to enter one of the last large, unsurveyed areas in the eastern United States and file for a homestead. Over thirteen hundred occupation permits were issued. However, with the renewal of Indian depredations in 1849, a precursor of events leading to the Third Seminole War (1855–58), most of these families abandoned the Indian River region. Following the Civil War, many of the former residents returned and, under terms of the 1862 Homestead Act which had absorbed the lands formerly covered by the Armed Occupation Act, reclaimed their homesteads. In addition to the former settlers, there was also an influx of families from all parts of the nation who were seeking a new start in Florida.

One of these was the Albert Lagow family of Illinois, which came by train from Vincennes, Indiana, to Jacksonville, thence by river steamer and wagon to the Indian River area. One of their daughters married a young river pilot, James Bell, and the couple settled at the hamlet of Fort Pierce in 1879. In her reminiscenses, *My Pioneer Days in Florida, 1876–1898*, published circa 1928,[18] Emily Lagow Bell provides one of the earliest histories of the Fort Pierce community; she also offers much valuable information about the interaction between the early white settlers and the Seminole Indians, primarily the Cow Creek band, who lived nearby and traded in the new towns springing up along the Indian River. One of her most interesting entries describes the arrival of the Hogg family, which established the first trading post and store at Fort Pierce:

"August the twenty-eight, 1879, we were so excited, for we saw a strange boat in sight, and we were so anxious we went to the bank of the creek and found they were going to land. Seven of us all lined up. A man came up the bank, then asked if they could camp there. Father Bell said certainly. It was Captain Benjamin Hogg, Mrs. Hogg and sons William, Alex, Marion. Later, his eldest daughter, Jessie came. . . .

17. Walter R. Hellier, *Indian River, Florida's Treasure Coast,* pp. 9–10. See also James W. Covington, "The Armed Occupation Act of 1842," pp. 41–52; John K. Mahon, *The Second Seminole War,* pp. 313–14.
18. This little book of reminiscences was privately published by the Old Timers' Association of Fort Pierce. One of the few remaining copies, signed by Emily Lagow Bell, is in the possession of Walter R. Hellier, who graciously loaned it to the author.

"Capt. Hogg said: 'Well, I have brought a load of groceries to sell or trade.'

"Father said: 'Fine, fine. You may have to stay for about ten days to send word to the cattlemen and Indians, for you can trade dry goods for hides to the Indians.'

"While the men talked we women folks talked. Mrs. Hogg said she bought one hundred dollars' worth of stuff on a fine watch and so they were going to try to build up with the country. We all became staunch friends. They were to run between Titusville and Jupiter. People came from Lake Worth to Jupiter to trade with them.

"Then the second trip they struck camp at old Fort Pierce and did a good business with the Indians. Captain built a palmetto house for their stuff. She had many ups and downs with the Indians. Those days brandied cherries and peaches were sold in all kinds of stores. So the Indians became very fond of them. So she would not keep them until she had some protection, for the Indians might get wild.

"We were so glad to have a store, even if it was two miles from us, and we felt we could have better eats. Capt. Hogg then bought a schooner and plied between Jacksonville and Fort Pierce. My husband was catching green turtle at that time, so Capt. Hogg took them there and sold them for him."[19]

In addition to such exotic items as green turtles and turtle eggs, Captain Hogg also reaped another harvest from the sea, for Bell reports that her family ". . . would go for miles to old wrecks and cut the copper bolts out of them and we would be miles from home, and carry them in sacks on our backs to get something to eat. Capt. Hogg would buy all we could get at fifteen cents a pound. Sometimes we would get fifty pounds, then go back the next day for more. As sometimes it would be all covered again, then we would have to dig the stuff out again."[20] Nevertheless, the major items of

---

19. Bell, *My Pioneer Days*, pp. 29–30. Although the Bell history is the only written account of the early days of the settlement, many of the incidents described therein are challenged by some of the older citizens of Fort Pierce. For example, Mrs. Annie Cobb, a granddaughter of Captain and Mrs. Hogg, claims that her family first came to the Indian River in 1874, not in 1879 as given by Bell. Ostensibly, the Hoggs first settled near present-day Sewall's Point in the Stuart area, but soon moved farther north to take advantage of the growing population and establish a store. For further information see interview with Mrs. Annie Cobb and Mr. Niels W. Jorgensen, Fort Pierce, February 8, 1973. Tape and transcript in University of Florida Indian Oral History Archives, Florida State Museum, Gainesville.

20. Bell, *My Pioneer Days*, p. 37.

trade at the Hogg store were the pelts and hides that white and
Indian hunters brought in from the back country. Sometime prior
to 1884, the Hoggs had built a permanent two-story building to
house their trading post.

The Hogg store and trading post became the gathering place for
the Indians when they came to Fort Pierce. They would make their
camps along the banks of Moore's Creek, and there were often several families at the site of the present-day Seventh Street park.
Emily Bell recounts that once she took her young son to the store,
and "who should I see but the store full of Indians, and I was so
scared I nearly lost my breath, but Mrs. Hogg gave me a chair
behind the counter and she could talk with some of them. Told old
Parker, he was chief at that time, I was Jim Bell's squaw. He said,
'Uncah Jimmie Bellegas pickaninny.' She nodded her head. Jim
Russell was there, so he said 'I will take you home. I go by there.'
And in the night my husband came home and I would not let him
in until he called me by name. I thought it Indians."[21] Evidently
this initial encounter took place during November of 1880 and was
the young white woman's first experience with the Seminoles. As
later accounts reveal, however, she soon became accustomed to
their presence, and they were welcomed into white homes on numerous occasions.

On one of their visits to the settlement, the Seminoles came to the
Bell home, with interesting results: "In 1882 they came in to the
river camp, and they would come to the house if the men folks were
there. I was baking some syrup cookies and had quite a large pan
full, looked up, and standing in the door were old Polly Parker, and
old Lucy and three children and old nigger Nance, who was Tusca-
nuga's wife. He was the ugliest human I have ever seen. Nance
was stolen when a child from St. Augustine. She never knew anything but Indians. Now I will tell you how they did me. I thought I
would pass them around. They would take two or three, but, no,
sir, old Polly took her dress up and poured the whole batch of them
in her dress, so the rest of them wouldn't get any, and I did not
know how to make them understand, and I heard my husband
whistling at the boat. So I motioned him to hurry and he saw the
guests I had. I told him. He made Polly give some to all of them.
She didn't like it. He told me to always divide with each one. I

21. Ibid., pp. 40–41.

learned to never have anything, for they liked to beg, but never would steal."[22]

Jim Bell had grown up on the Florida frontier among the Seminoles and had good rapport with them; his wife remembered that "My husband had been with them for ten years. He and his father, his brother, Frank, could understand them and talk to them."[23] When the second Bell child came along, the family was so well-adjusted to having Indians about that the youngster would learn to accept Seminole children as playmates. Emily Bell's account recorded that "I had a little girl baby. Her name was Madge, and the little Indians would play with her and her brother, Charles. They were their first playmates, friends too. My husband and Henry Parker were great boy friends, go swimming together and hunting. He was a fine large Indian and a favorite with the whites. He was standing on the bank at Ten Mile Creek when his dog must have jumped up and struck the trigger of his gun and it went off and killed him. He was about 20 years old. They all mourned for him."[24]

It is likely that many of the Seminole people who had adopted the name "Parker" did so because of their contact with a white trader named Henry Parker who moved into the Kissimmee River valley about 1870–71.[25] He first built and operated a ferry at Bluff Hammock, then later moved farther down the river to a site near Fort Bassenger. This was sold to Rabon Raulerson of Bartow in 1873, and Parker moved on again to Fort Drum. Here he built a double-pen log house and a store and trading post. Parker's store became a trading post for the Seminoles where they could obtain groceries, guns, ammunition, and other supplies in exchange for alligator, deer, and otter hides, alligator teeth, and bird plumes. This trading post apparently ceased to function around the turn of the century.

In 1883 the Bell family held an old-time Christmas celebration replete with a tree decorated with candles; there was also a party and dance with about two dozen residents in attendance. In describing the party Mrs. Bell wrote, "Oh! I was about to forget my

22. Ibid., p. 41.
23. Ibid.
24. Ibid.
25. *Tampa Tribune*, December 13, 1959, p. 4E. A personal account of Henry Parker's trading post was given to the author by Mrs. Addie H. Emerson of Fort Pierce, who spent her early years in the Fort Drum area. Mrs. Emerson's grandmother was Parker's second wife. Some of Mrs. Emerson's comments are recorded on the Cobb-Jorgensen taped interview.

husband had an accordion and there were two Indians with us—
Dr. Johnnie and Billy Bowlegs. Billy said he could play it, so someone gave it to him, and they told him to play 'Leather Breeches,'
and he said 'encah,' so started, and he played the same thing until
we were nearly distracted. So I said, 'For heaven's sake, give him
something to eat and get that thing and hide it.' We could hear the
violin then."[26] There were also less humorous incidents, such as the
time the Seminoles were riled over the theft of their hogs and cattle
by some white men, and the Bells were asked to intercede with the
Indians to prevent bloodshed; "the next morning my husband and
his father and brother, all good friends with the Indians, said they
would try to settle for them. They got over to Fort Pierce and had
to raise two hundred dollars. That was their price. It was something
hard to get that, but finally settled it, and the rustlers got the cattle,
all right, but some of them had to leave the country. We were glad
to see the men alive to get back to us. We gave a shout, and for
weeks we were shaky, for we didn't understand Indians."[27] In one
respect, it is remarkable that the Seminoles did not get more worked
up than they did over attempts by various whites to defraud them
and take their property. Some of the settlers in the region never did
accept the presence of the Indians and took every opportunity to
bilk them if possible; there were also those who came from outside
the region for the purpose of making their fortune at the expense
of the Indians. Bell's history notes one such instance after her parents had opened a boarding house in 1886: "Mother had six men
boarders. Of course, we didn't know their business then, but some
bought hides, others came for health, and one man, Mr. Roy, was
trying to get to trade with the Indians, get deer hides for whiskey.
So father told him the government men would get him. He did not
tarry very long. Next boat he left."[28] Evidently Mrs. Lagow, Emily
Bell's mother, also became a good friend of the Seminole people,
for as the narrative continues, "Their boarders thought it wonderful
that mother could get such a meal. She would fix palmetto cabbage
and they said it was better than green corn, and where did she get
the turkeys and deer meat? She said: 'You will see the ones who are
the hunters.'

"Mother knew the Indians would be in that night. Sure enough,

26. Bell, *My Pioneer Days,* pp. 41–42.
27. Ibid., p. 43.
28. Ibid., pp. 46–47.

there was Henry Parker, Johnny Doctor and Polly and Lucy at the door early.

"The drummers stood back and watched them. All brought some kind of meats, but mother always took a sharp knife and cut a thin layer all over it off. She said they always looked so dirty.

"Mother told the boarders she doctored them when they were sick. They liked her."[29]

By 1890, Annie Hogg had sold out to a group of men from Connecticut who came to start an oyster cannery operation that they called "Cantown." The president of the company was Julius Tyler, and he was assisted by Peter P. Cobb, who had formerly been associated with the store while it was owned by the Hoggs.[30] The store was restocked, and when the canning operation failed, Cobb bought the entire operation. Cobb was appointed postmaster at Fort Pierce in 1888. He continued to do business at the same location on the river front until the 1930s, and welcomed the Seminoles as his customers. The tale is told of one occasion when the Indian squaws got what they thought was a can of baking powder and made biscuits with it; when they all later became ill it was discovered that the can actually contained arsenic used to poison rats. One Indian youngster became violently ill, and despite efforts to get him to a doctor in Melbourne the child died; he was buried in what is now a public park. Mr. Cobb and others tried to have the park named Osceola after the family of the child, but to no avail.[31] Finally, the trading post was closed when Mr. Cobb became too infirm to run it, and he had no heirs to leave it to upon his death. The original building still stands in Fort Pierce, a visible link with its trading past, and in one sense a monument to the friendly relations between the Seminoles and local townspeople that has existed since the 1870s.

The small community of White City, located some five miles below Fort Pierce on the St. Lucie River, also shared in the Indian trade. In the 1890s, a colony of Danish-Americans settled there,

29. Ibid.
30. Ibid., pp. 30–31. Here, also, Mrs. Cobb disputes the assertion of Emily Lagow Bell that Peter Cobb had been associated with the Hogg store and trading post prior to the arrival of the cannery company. Yet, there are no factual data showing just when Mr. Cobb did arrive in Fort Pierce, only that he was appointed postmaster in 1888. Presumably he was in possession of the store at that time and used part of it as the post office for the community.
31. Hellier, Indian River, p. 28.

drawn by glowing accounts of Florida in *The Danish Pioneer* news-paper, and encouraged by the Flagler interests which owned the tract of land. Most of these Danes were from the midwest and had attended the Chicago World's Fair of 1890; they were impressed with the section of the fair known as White City, and named their new community after it. The first male child born in the colony was Niels W. Jorgensen.[32] This native son has compiled a narrative his-tory of the Danish colony based on his own experiences and the ac-counts of the original settlers; some of his fondest memories as a boy growing up on the Florida frontier centered on contacts with the Indians. His family lived on Midway Road west of the river, which was sort of a gateway to the south and west, as an old army road or trail dating from the Seminole wars ran about a mile west of the town. This military road linked Jupiter on the south with Okeechobee City and the Bassenger–Fort Drum region to the north-west. Before the railroad came to Okeechobee City in 1915, this road had been the main artery for fruit growers bringing their produce to the railroad for shipment north. It was a high, dry roadway, and a sturdy bridge spanned the St. Lucie River at a point west of White City. The Seminoles also preferred this route even when going on to Fort Pierce with their wagons loaded with pelts and hides, but many stopped to trade with the Scandinavian community.

Since the Jorgensens lived on the edge of town, they were the first whites that the Indians saw, and Niels' mother felt at first that they were not friendly. Then one day a Seminole asked his father if he could borrow the family horse and buggy to take a sick child to the doctor in Fort Pierce; the elder Jorgensen agreed, and after the Indian returned the rig, he later brought in venison and became quite friendly with the family. The only time that there was any ten-sion between the whites and Indians that Jorgensen can recall, came in 1907 as a result of the incident in which the remains of Captain Tom Tiger were removed and taken north by a promoter.[33] The people became alarmed as word spread that the Seminoles were go-ing on the warpath, and plans were made to defend the settlement. Even young Niels, who owned a single-shot 22 rifle, was given an extra box of cartridges. Fortunately, the rumors of eminent attack were quieted by Sheriff Dan Carlton and other prominent settlers

32. Niels William Jorgensen, "History of White City" (typescript). Mr. Jorgensen supplemented this account with the taped interview cited.
33. Jorgensen Manuscript, p. 4.

who reasoned with the Seminoles and worked to have the bones returned to their rightful place. Although the local press made capital of statements by the Indian medicine man Billy Smith and others, Jorgensen's report that the Seminoles said "No fight white man, too many" probably reflects a more realistic stance. In the end, the situation which had so greatly distressed the Cow Creek band was apparently settled to their satisfaction.

When the Seminoles came to White City, they traded primarily at the stores operated by Tom Howard and Jim Orell. They arrived every two or three months with loads of alligator hides, raccoon skins and otter pelts which they traded, an item at a time, for coffee, flour, sugar, dry goods, or anything striking their fancy. On one occasion a group of Seminole squaws entered one of the stores and became quite taken with a display of child-size agate chamber pots; after much discussion they decided that these would make ideal cooking vessels, and purchased the entire supply. Not all of the white man's inventions struck their fancy at first, and it is reported that the Seminole comment on the first bicycles that they saw in town was "White man heap lazy, sitting down walking."[34] However, the Seminoles were fond of beads, coffee grinders, and many other articles that were often in short supply at the stores, and Jorgensen recalls ordering many items for them from Sears, Roebuck & Co. catalogs.

The Seminoles were always considered excellent hunters. During one extremely dry year, about 1908, a family of Indians camped in the savannah west of the city and took over eighty alligators in one week. In their hunting and trapping activities the Seminoles increasingly came into competition with an itinerant element of white hunters who made their living the same way, and this often led to ill-will; yet, there did not seem to be any overt discrimination in the prices paid to white and Indian hunters for their goods. Jorgensen recalls that "an otter skin was worth up to $25.00 and if a man shipped his hides, a raccoon brought up to $1.50 per hide."[35] If the skins were sold to the stores, the raccoon might bring forty cents and the otter pelts only three to five dollars. "Alligator hides were sold by the foot with a minimum length of three feet which brought the lowest price and a maximum of 7 feet with maximum price. A hide over 7 feet would bring no more than a seven footer which brought

34. Ibid.
35. Ibid., p. 15.

about $1.50 salted."[36] This price for an alligator hide could, of course, fluctuate radically with the demand for alligator products in the fashion markets. After 1912 there was apparently a great drop in the hide market which severely affected the Seminoles and other hunters. Nevertheless, the price of $1.50 for a seven-foot gator hide is substantially higher than at the turn of the century when the going price was approximately ten cents per foot paid to the hunter.

Jorgensen knew and hunted with Billy Smith, the Seminole medicine man who lived in the Bluefield district west of Fort Pierce. He always found the Indians courteous and willing to share their camp and food with whites that they knew, and he felt that they were always well accepted by the people in the town. This view is shared by many other old-timers in the lower Indian River trading region.

36. Ibid.

7

The Southwest Frontier Trade

GEORGE W. Storter was born in Germany in 1829 and emigrated to this country with his family when he was six years of age. His parents died during an epidemic of yellow fever, and the youngster was raised by a Frenchman living in the New Orleans area. As a young man he moved to Eutau, Alabama, and became a tinsmith, married a young lady from Mississippi, and settled down to raise a family. However, the Civil War intervened, and Storter served throughout the conflict as a member of the 4th Alabama Cavalry. After he returned home from the war, his wife passed away. Storter was suffering from asthma, and so he decided to move south and make a new start in Florida. In the summer of 1877 he arrived, with his sons George and R. B., at the Pine Level community near Fort Winder, not far from the present town of Arcadia. The trip had taken over a month by mule-drawn covered wagon.

During the fall of 1881, the senior Storter sailed to the Ten Thousand Islands region to farm with William S. Allen at his place on Allen's River. They raised crops of cucumbers, tomatoes, and eggplants for the produce markets in Key West and New York. The Storter sons arrived in February of 1882 to help with the harvest but returned to the Fort Winder area with their father in the spring of that year. They found only three inhabited spots along the route their schooner took: Joe Wiggins' small trading post and apiary at Wiggins Pass, Capt. W. T. Collier's dock at Marco, and the telegraph station at Punta Rassa where they landed. Although the southwest frontier was virtually uninhabited and had a forbidding climate, it also had rich soil and presented great opportunity for men who were willing to take the risks involved. In 1883, Storter and his youngest son, R. B. (called Bembery), returned to Allen's River and took up a claim down the river from Mr. Allen. The young George W. Storter did not join them until 1887 when he brought his wife and infant daughter to the settlement. His first job was cutting buttonwood by the cord to supply the Key West stove-wood market; next he successfully took up farming crops of eggplants, then sugarcane. The Storters built a mill to grind the cane to syrup, and their father plied his trade as tinsmith making containers for the liquid. Apparently all of these ventures profited, for when William S. Allen died in 1889, young George was able to purchase his entire holding along the river for $800, and he moved into the old Allen homestead.[1] The settlement was later given the name Everglade.

In 1892, Capt. George W. Storter took out a $1.50 occupational license to open a general store serving the few settlers in the area; it also became a trading post for the Mikasuki-speaking Seminoles who lived in the region.[2] When Storter first came to Allen's River, there were no Indians around; but in the 1880s five canoeloads moved into the lower Big Cypress Swamp to make their camps. Storter always believed that the Indians had moved back north because there was no readily accessible trading post on the river. Although Joe Wiggins had operated his trading post and apiary at Wiggins Pass around 1880, he soon moved to Allen's River and opened another store. When Wiggins moved again, this time to Sand Fly Pass, the store was bought by a Mr. Lennart of Tampa, who operated it only a month. Thus, by 1886 there was no trading post on the easily navigable Allen's River, and Storter took advantage of this opportunity. The original building had a dirt floor, homemade shelves and counters, and an open screen front with a canvas curtain to keep out the rain and cold.[3] Later, a permanent wooden store and warehouse, with attached post office, was built near the Storter home. There was a tin shop out back for old G. W. Storter, and a boat haul track for scraping and repairing vessels; a separate building on the dock was used to store fuel and alligator hides awaiting shipment. The family operated the store until 1922, and

1. Tebeau, *Florida's Last Frontier*, p. 116.
2. Interview with Mr. Kirby Storter, Miami, Sept. 15, 1971. Tape and transcript in University of Florida Indian Oral History Archives, Florida State Museum, Gainesville.
3. Tebeau, *Florida's Last Frontier*, p. 117.

during that time approximately half of their customers were "Cypress Indians." The Storters had not heard the term "Mikasuki" until this century, but they apparently differentiated this group of Indians from the Seminole people living further north in the region around Lake Okeechobee.

Because of the isolation of Everglade, supplies for the store had to be brought in by schooner from Key West and Tampa. R. B. Storter was in charge of the family shipping interests, and his fifty-foot schooner the *Bertie Lee*, named for his brother's oldest daughter, was well known in South Florida waters at the turn of the century. A post office was established at the settlement in 1895, and it was R. B. who suggested the name of Everglade. The following year he received the first contract to haul mail from Everglade to Key West for $1,100 per year. His son recalls that "he used to carry supplies to Key West in every Tuesday, returning on Friday or Saturday, sometimes Sunday if the wind and weather were not good for sailing. The main cargo of the *Bertie Lee* was salt mullet, shipped on to Cuba from Key West, chickens, eggs, peppers, tomatoes, pumpkins, sugarcane, syrup, potatoes, oysters, cord buttonwood, lemons, limes, and hogs. I will never forget the mixture of smells that came from the deck of the boat when it was loaded and ready to sail. Families in the area brought their goods to my father to be taken to Key West and sold. My Aunt Toogie would send her hot pepper sauce and sell it for 15¢ a bottle. They were the same peppers that were stuck to my tongue when I said a bad word. . . . My father, besides taking goods to Key West, took alligator hides to Bayer Brothers in Tampa once a month. The area thrived with an abundance of crops, wild animals, and plenty of good fish."[4] Bembery Storter had three other schooners after the *Bertie Lee* was wrecked and also operated the forty-foot power launch *Terre Haute*, which was used to take the Storter children to high school in Fort Myers. However, his primary function was the crucial one of getting supplies into Everglade and taking off the produce and trade goods brought in by the settlers and Indians.

The Indians brought in a variety of trade goods to the Storter store: otter and raccoon pelts, bee's wax, lemon seed, fresh venison and turkey, cured buckskin, and some Indian handicrafts such as dolls, dresses, sofkee spoons, and carved canoes for the winter

4. R. L. Storter, *Seventy-Seven Years at Everglades, Chokoloskee, Naples,* pp. 14, 19.

tourist trade.[5] A common item of trade was alligator hides, which the Indians brought in salted and rolled. There were also small 'gators which had been skinned out in their entirety for souvenirs, and these brought a slightly higher price. The hides were packed in empty sugar barrels and stored in a building adjacent to the store until there were enough to ship out to Bayer Brothers' warehouse. Some months the Storter store handled as many as seven hundred alligator hides. There were also many alligator hides brought in by white hunters in the Everglades. There is a story told of one extremely hot summer when the land was so dry that a wagon could be driven all over the Everglades, and the alligators were clustered in small lakes or ponds. A hunter named Roberts found a lake teeming with the reptiles and a number of hunters participated in the kill; that summer R. B. Storter carried over 10,000 hides from Everglade.[6] The Indians also brought in plumes to trade with Storter. At first he was not sure of their value, but finally agreed to pay fifty cents for poor ones and seventy-five cents for those of better quality. When Storter had collected enough to stuff a mattress, he took them to Key West where they were sold for a handsome profit. About that time, plumes were reportedly bringing as much as five dollars each on the open market.

The Seminoles were waited on individually in Storter's store, and since they arrived several canoeloads at a time, it could take as long as twelve hours to complete a trading session. The Indians were paid in cash for the goods that they brought in. They paid for an item at a time. Thus the Indian would have his goods, and the Storters would have their money back, and the process would begin again with another Seminole. In this manner the shortage of cash money at the trading post was easily overcome. Only rarely did the Indians not spend their entire income before leaving the store; but if they did have a cash surplus, they would refuse paper money, since it was subject to rotting or mutilation in the camps. Gold and silver coins were relatively indestructible, and they could also be strung together as ornamental necklaces or bracelets. On occasion Indians sought to buy on credit, which they called "make book," and it was usually granted since the majority always honored their debts.[7]

5. Storter interview.
6. Charlton W. Tebeau, *The Story of the Chokoloskee Bay Country*, p. 48.
7. Storter interview.

Most of the "Cypress Indians" understood English, and there was little difficulty in communicating. The Storters also learned enough of the Mikasuki language, particularly idioms and the names of store goods, to facilitate trade. The Indians bought mainly groceries, especially coffee, flour, salt, and grits, which they used in making "sofkee." Different kinds of cloth, and hand-cranked sewing machines each costing about twenty-five dollars, were popular among the women, as were multi-hued glass beads which were sold for $1.75 a pound and sometimes more. Early in the twentieth century the men began buying trousers. Often they would stuff their knee-length shirts in at the waist, giving a rather rumpled appearance. Derby hats and broad-brimmed woven hats were also popular. The Storters did not regularly stock guns, but these could be ordered from suppliers in Tampa.[8] The Knight & Wall hardware company was a major source of rifles, ammunition, and other such items. The most popular weapon among the Seminoles was the Winchester '38, 1873 model, lever action, which was very effective in bringing down deer or dispatching an alligator. Twelve- and sixteen-gauge shotguns and twenty-two-gauge pump-action rifles were also used, and it was easy to obtain ammunition for them. After completing their trading, the Indians often remained overnight in the loft of the store or made camp on the grounds. Only once did an Indian abuse the hospitality by attempting to steal from the store during the night; his name was Brown Tiger, and he was barred from further commerce at Everglade.[9]

Capt. George Storter's family consisted of nine children, six girls and three boys, while his brother R. B. had three girls and six boys. These children growing up around the trading post at Everglade had a great deal of interaction with the Indians, and two of them have left extensive accounts of those days.[10] Apparently there was a great variation in the physical make-up and stature of the Indians, some families being tall and robust, such as Tom Billie's, while the family of Billy Conapatchee was short, averaging only about 5'4" or 5'5" in height. There was also great variation in the length of the "long shirts" worn by the males; some were ankle-length with gaudy

8. Ibid.
9. Ibid. See also D. G. Copeland, "Data Relative to Florida" (typescript), p. 1136.
10. R. L. Storter, the son of R. B. "Bembery" Storter, and Kirby Storter, a son of Capt. George W. Storter, have both left accounts of their younger days in and around the Everglades region.

striping, while others were plain white and very short, coming well above the knee. While this loose-fitting shirt was comfortable and utilitarian for hunting and camping in wet country, it also had certain disadvantages. One day a short, stout Indian by the name of Charlie Doctor was working in a sugarcane field when a bee flew up his dress and delivered a sting, and he took off down the row screaming and yelling "bumble bee" in his own language. On other occasions the Indians seemed impervious to pain. Captain Storter kept a pair of forceps which he used to extract teeth between visits by a regular dentist, and he served both whites and Indians. In those days, of course, there was no Novocain available at the store, and the Storter children began to panic whenever a tooth had to come out. The Indians, however, would sit passively while Storter worried with the tooth, and when it finally came out they would emit only an "Uh!" and then walk away.

The Indians who came to Everglade were basically honest and peaceful, but they were quite fond of whiskey. There were some of them who engaged in making "moonshine," and a fellow named Water Turkey turned out a particularly potent hundred-proof product. They occasionally hid their bottles and jugs up under the Storter house, which was elevated some six feet off the ground to avoid high water.

Old Charlie Tommie was an Indian whose feet showed the scars of numerous snake bites, and he told the youngest Storter boy that the first time he was bitten by some type of moccasin, not a cottonmouth, that he was "sick, sick, sick" for about three weeks; later he was bitten and sick for about a week; the third time he was sick for about three days; "next time," he said, "no sick."[11]

Young Bruce Storter was ordinarily in charge of getting the Indians organized to pose for pictures for tourists who came to Everglade. In their colorful costumes and brightly painted canoes, the Seminoles were a favorite subject for picture postcards from Florida early in this century. One time the Indians balked, for a reason lost to posterity, and Bruce induced them to return with gifts of cheap cigars and bits of tobacco. From that point on, he was the intermediary at picture taking time.

In his little book *Seventy-Seven Years at Everglades, Chokoloskee, Naples,* R. L. Storter, one of R. B.'s sons, recalls, "My sisters, brothers, cousins and I swam in the river every chance we got. We made

11. Storter interview.

boats out of whatever we could find. Often we played hide-in-seek in the cane fields, chased fiddler crabs and hung our feet overboard to let the catfish suck on our toes. We were healthy children and didn't need a doctor often. . . . One day while swimming in the Everglade River my cousin and I almost got caught by this thirteen foot alligator. I ran and got a gun and peppered him with three loads of shot. Another time an alligator did catch a dog and kill it. These were rare occasions however. Most of the alligators I saw were skinned in my uncle's store or on the schooner. . . . I can remember my uncle measuring gator hides an entire day and the schooner being loaded down with them."[12] Yet, life at Everglade was not all play for the younger children, for in 1893 a school was started in a bedroom of the Storter home. A teacher was sent out by Monroe County, and a school building was ready for the 1895–96 school year. Then in 1902 it was discovered, as a result of the Shands Survey of disputed territory, that Everglade was actually in Lee County. Thereafter Lee County supplied the teacher and replaced the school building after it was destroyed in the hurricane of 1910. At one time the oldest Storter daughter, Bertie Lee, served as teacher at the school. There is no record of any "Cypress Indians" ever wanting to attend the school to learn to read and write English.

In the late 1880s, the Florida Conference of the Methodist Church sent the Reverend George W. Gatewood to survey the mission field in the Ten Thousand Islands region. His positive report was responsible for having the first minister sent into the region, and Gatewood returned a year or so later as the permanent pastor at Everglade. He resided in the home of Captain Storter until his marriage in 1892, and when the first Methodist Church was built, the Storter brothers served as church officers. The Reverend Gatewood recalled that the first trading establishment for Indians was the one that Joe Wiggins opened, followed by the Storter store. "At these stores," he wrote, "the Indians traded or sold their hides and furs and bought their supplies. The merchant, though, had to first pay the Indians in cash for what they had to sell, and then the Indians would start buying and pay for each article as it was wrapped up."[13]

During Gatewood's tenure at Everglade he got to know most of the Seminole people who frequented the store and often invited

12. R. L. Storter, *Seventy-Seven Years*, p. 25.
13. George W. Gatewood, *Ox Cart Days to Airplane Era in Southwest Florida*, p. 29.

them to dine with him at home. Although most of the males wore only the traditional long shirt costume, Gatewood recounted that one of the Indians liked to wear long pants when he visited the store and hid a pair near the head of Allen's River so that he could change before coming in to trade. One time some other Indians found the trousers and hid them, so the Indian had to come "in his shirttail."[14] The Seminole to whom he was referring was Miami Billy, the brother of Billy Conapatchee and Billy Fewell, and Gatewood thought he took the incident philosophically—which was not his style. Other Indians that the minister recalled were Squirrel Jumper, Water Turkey, Tommy Osceola, and Johnny Osceola, who "sometimes would wrestle with the white boys who were willing to tackle him."[15]

When the little Methodist Church was built, the services were open to all, and Mr. Gatewood wrote, "I remember having the Indians for part of my congregation. The Indians, though, when they came in refused to sit on the benches and sat cross-legged on the floor. They would sit there throughout the service."[16] Although they attended church and apparently enjoyed the service, especially the singing, no Seminole ever showed any interest in conversion to Christianity. They were apparently satisfied with their own beliefs and values well into this century.

To a degree, Captain Storter himself became a part of the Indian folklore, due no doubt in part to the key role that he played in sustaining their life style. Once he engaged Johnny Osceola in a dialogue concerning Seminole beliefs about debt and the life hereafter, and must have been surprised to find himself prominently featured. As reported by D. G. Copeland, the conversation went as follows:

"No pay one year, all right; no pay two year, get other Injuns with big sticks in line, make him run between, hit one time for every dollar."
"Little Billy, he pay me?"
"Uncah [yes], he good injun, he pay."
"Billy Tommy pay me, think so?"
"Dunno, lazy ojus [plenty], no hunt. Injun just like white man, some pay, some no pay, some good, some holowaugus (bad) to hell."

14. Ibid.
15. Ibid.
16. Ibid., p. 30.

"Think so bad Injun go Happy Hunting Ground?"

"No! Me think so, Injun after Big Sleep, come to big river with pole across it, pole pretty slick, bad Injun fall off, alpate (alligator) catch him. Good Injun get across pole to Happy Hunting Ground."

"You think white man Happy Hunting Ground like Indian?"

"Unca, Injun hunt alpate, sell him George Storter, same as here."

"You think Injun ever fight white man any more?"

"No use, white man all round, Injun in middle."[17]

Storter may have been instrumental in getting the Indians to begin making the famous Seminole dolls for the South Florida tourist trade, although it is popularly thought that the late Deaconess Harriett Bedell was the prime mover in reviving tribal handicrafts during the 1930s and '40s.[18] As the story was told by E. F. Coe, writing in 1921, "The Seminole boys and girls have very few playthings. The boys early in life leave off playing with toys; the girls have few play things. About twenty years ago, a Convention of Doll Land was held in New York City and Capt. Geo. Storter was requested by the lady who was conducting same, to furnish specimen of dolls made by the Indians (Seminoles) and upon inquiry from them, they said 'Sometimes we make 'em, but think so make 'em dolls, Indian get sick,' but Mr. Storter prevailed upon them to make specimens of Indian dolls, which were exhibited at this Doll Land Convention and they are still on exhibition there. There are only two Seminole Indians who are making these dolls—specimens of which were brought back by visitors to the camp. The body of the doll is made of a piece of cypress or other soft material and the face is sculptured out with an ordinary pocket knife. The black dye illustrates the hair, eyes and ears of the doll, and are dyes which cannot be easily removed. . . . Mr. Storter succeeded in having a Seminole Indian make a small canoe with the Indian Chief standing erect therein, properly gowned in his vari-colored shirt, with his squaw seated in the bottom of the canoe, each of whom are dressed in typical Indian garb. A specimen of this product has been on exhibition at Knights and Walls store in Tampa."[19] It is also recalled by a Storter

17. A. W. Dimock and Julian A. Dimock, *Florida Enchantments*, p. 314.
18. William Hartley and Ellen Hartley, *A Woman Set Apart*, passim.
19. E. F. Coe, "Seminole Tips" (typescript, 1921), in Copeland, "Data Relative to Florida," 2:726.

son that these Indian handicrafts became popular items to sell to northern tourists visiting Everglade during the winter season.

Early in this century, Everglade had become a popular resort for winter visitors, particularly sportsmen who appreciated the great fishing and hunting of the region. To accommodate this influx, Storter made additions to his family home, and this in turn became the nucleus of the famous Rod and Gun Club that still operates at Everglades City. Among the tourists attracted to South Florida was the streetcar advertising magnate Barron G. Collier, who ultimately settled in Lee County. In 1921 he purchased the first of land holdings that would ultimately exceed one million acres in Lee, Hendry, and Collier Counties—the latter created by a legislative act in 1923 and named for the largest land owner. A key acquisition by the Collier interests came in 1922, when George Storter sold his holding at Everglade. The following year the town was renamed Everglades City and became the county seat of the new Collier County. The old Storter home temporarily became the first county courthouse, and George W. Storter served as chairman of the first board of county commissioners from 1923 to 1925.[20] He then resigned to become county judge, and held that position until 1928, the year before his death. When the Storters sold their store on Allen's River, later renamed Barron's River in honor of the egocentric new owner, the remaining Indian trade shifted completely to Chokoloskee Island.

Chokoloskee Island, less than 150 acres in extent and rising only twenty feet above sea level, lies in the shallow inland sea known as Chokoloskee Bay, some six miles southeast of Everglades City.[21] Since 1955 it has been reached by a causeway and bridge from the mainland, but for most of this century shallow-draft vessels brought in supplies and mail and carried out the produce raised by the islanders for the Key West market. Although various families had settled on the island for varying lengths of time since the 1870s, it was really put on the map by C. G. McKinney, who arrived in 1886. McKinney engaged in farming and ran a small store or trading post which catered to the few white settlers and Seminole Indians who poled their canoes down from the Big Cypress region. In 1891 a post office was established through the efforts of McKinney, who became the first postmaster. For a few months he called the post

20. Dedication Brochure, Collier County Court House, East Naples, 1962.
21. Tebeau, *Chokoloskee Bay Country*, p. 5.

office "Comfort" but then changed it to "Chokoloskee" after the island; several years later George W. Storter wanted to name his post office on Allen's River "Chokoloskee," but when he found that McKinney had preempted the name he used "Everglade" instead.

Mr. and Mrs. Dan House of Naples spent most of their early years on Chokoloskee Island and well recall the Indians who came there to trade. Willie House was one of McKinney's daughters and often worked in her father's store taking in furs from Seminoles such as Josie Billie and Willie Willie, among others. The Indian families would come in at irregular intervals and make camp on the beach in front of McKinney's store while they traded pelts and hides for silver and gold coins; they then bought groceries, traps, ammunition, and rifles, as well as other necessities for survival in the wilderness. After the trading had been concluded, the Indians might remain for several days, eating, drinking, and generally enjoying their visit to the settlement. There was always a pot of "sofkee" on the fire in the camps—now made from grits instead of coontie flour—and the men ate first using a common spoon. This change was one evidence of the Indian's growing dependence on the white man's store goods. Interestingly, in a sense this brought the Florida Seminoles full circle to their Creek origins, where hominy grits were utilized in making "sofkee." To prepare hominy the Indians soaked hard, dry-stored corn in lye water created by using wood ashes, which expanded and softened the grain. Wet or dry, the corn was pounded to flour (grits) in a traditional log mortar. The product was then sifted in baskets to remove the hard outer skin or hull. This process was adapted to preparing the coontie (Zamia) by the Seminoles.

Apparently the Seminoles paid the same price for store items as did the islanders (prices were high), and little credit was granted to anyone. McKinney's billhead bore the statement "No Banking, No Mortgaging, No Insurance, No Borrowing, No Loaning. I must have cash to buy more hash."[22] Many of the supplies for the island stores were brought in by Dan House on his fifty-two-foot schooner *Rosina*, which he regularly ran to Key West, although hardware items such as guns and plows were ordered out of Knight & Wall Co. in Tampa.

Dan House was born in Arcadia in 1889, but his family moved to the Chokoloskee Bay country when he was about eight years old, settling first on Turner River and later moving to the island. Al-

22. Ibid., p. 22.

though he received only intermittent schooling (a 1905 photo shows him attending the elementary school on the island), he personified the rugged individualism of the islanders who resorted to numerous strategies to earn a living. At one time or another he worked as farmer, fisherman, trapper, hunter, tanner, guide, and Indian trader to make ends meet.[23] House was friendly with the Seminoles and occasionally took a canoe-load of groceries into the Everglades and Big Cypress to trade for hides. He recalls that a 'coon hide would bring from twenty-five to seventy-five cents, while otter pelts were worth from eight to ten dollars apiece. Seven-foot alligators were worth $1.25 to House, who would resell them to Southern Hide & Skins Co. in Jacksonville for approximately $1.75—a relatively small profit to the trader for his efforts. Later, House became a buyer for Charles Mann, who owned the Jacksonville firm, and he remembers having as many as 2,500 'coon skins stacked on his porch (many from white hunters) awaiting shipment. Alligator skins were packed in barrels for shipment, but House took 'coon and otter skins to Naples by boat, from whence they were transported to Jacksonville by automobile in what must have been an olfactory calamity for the driver in hot, humid weather.

House made his greatest profit around the turn of the century in the plume trade, buying egret feathers from the Seminoles for three to five dollars each and selling them to tourists for five to ten dollars for a particularly good spray.[24] This trade, of course, came to an end after the passage of anti-pluming laws and the waning of fashion demands for feathers. Another high profit item was rough lemon seed which the Indians brought in from hammock groves; House paid them five dollars a quart for the lemon seed and sold it to grove nurserymen for ten dollars a quart for use in growing grafting stock for other citrus. Very few items were overlooked by the islanders, and Mrs. House remembers that her mother paid children one-fourth cent each for grasshoppers, which she sold for one and one-fourth cents each to the American Entomological Co. in Brooklyn, N.Y. There was a similar market for wasps, bees, beetles, etc. which were shipped packed in a formaldehyde solution. Willie House, like so many other women of the region, also did her share

23. Interview with Mr. and Mrs. Dan House, Naples, July 8, 1972. Tape and transcript in University of Florida Indian Oral History Archives, Florida State Museum, Gainesville.
24. Ibid.

of plume hunting, fishing, and other chores ordinarily thought of as "man's work"; they were valuable contributors to the economic survival of their families.

One Indian who was quite friendly with Dan House was old Charlie Tigertail, who had his own little trading post on a canoe run in the Everglades. He had started out with a five-horsepower engine on a canoe to carry supplies into the interior; however, this didn't work out, so he had George Storter build him a flatbottom boat complete with a cabin and roll-down canvas window covers.[25] Occasionally Tigertail and other Indians would leave items under the House's porch for safekeeping, and once Dan found a buried tin can of money. He feared that if someone came along and stole it, Tigertail would blame him, so he took it into the house for safety until the Indians' next visit—and sure enough, the Indian came looking for his "bank" as expected. The Indians were not alone in burying their money in the sand beneath houses, and no matter how tightly the lids were placed on the mason jars, the coins always seemed to turn green. In the late 1920s, the Indian trade was past its zenith, C. G. McKinney had passed away, and the store was no longer in the family, so Dan and Willie House left the island to make their home in Naples, where they still reside on House Street —named in their honor. Dan House also had the distinction of being related by marriage to both of the major traders on Chokoloskee Island, since his older sister married Ted Smallwood, whose trading post became the center of island commerce.

C. S. "Ted" Smallwood was born in North Florida in 1873, but like so many others of that period, he eventually made his way to the southwestern area of the state seeking economic opportunities. After extensive travel about the southern tip of the peninsula and into the Bahama Islands, Smallwood finally settled in the Chokoloskee Bay region in the 1890s and took up farming with D. D. House. He soon married Mamie House, and the couple established a residence on the east side of the island; by 1903 Smallwood and his father had become the leading landowners there, and he built the family residence on the south side of the island that was occupied for over half a century. In 1906 he opened a trading post and store in his home, which was set back on high ground about one hundred yards from the water's edge. The same year he succeeded C. G. McKinney as postmaster and moved the post office to the same location; Small-

25. Ibid.

wood retained that post until his retirement in 1941, and then his daughter Thelma became the postmistress of the island. The business at Smallwood's Store flourished and, as Tebeau has noted, "after 1906 the Smallwood place became increasingly the trading headquarters for the region, being rivaled only by that of Captain George W. Storter, Jr., at Everglades."[26] After the Storters sold their holdings to Barron Collier in 1922, Smallwood's Store was indeed the major Indian trading post in Southwest Florida.

When the trade operation became too large for the Smallwood home, a store was built at the shoreline in 1917, and the following year a channel was dredged to allow larger craft to reach the store dock. The shallow waters of Chokoloskee Bay offered a safe inland passage for boats plying the coastal waters, as well as for Indian canoes; with the addition of the channel, larger vessels could also take advantage of the Smallwood location. The hurricane of 1924 set the store awash and moved it some six inches off its foundation, so the following year Ted Smallwood had it raised some ten feet off the ground on pilings—just in time to avoid the devastating waters of the 1926 hurricane. The store was operated by Smallwood for thirty-five years, and it is still open to the public under the management of his daughter, who has made it a major tourist attraction on the island.

As a youngster growing up around her father's trading post, Thelma Smallwood had numerous contacts with the Seminole families who came to trade there; in an interview with Tebeau she gave a full account of those activities:

> The Indians used to come in here and camp on the beach. At Christmas time there might be a hundred Indians. The men would all get drunk but one. He would bring their knives, guns, etc., in the store for my father to put under the counter until they got sober. When I was small some of the Indians would bring eight-pound lard buckets full of silver coins to my father to keep until they needed the money. They did not like paper money. One time my father gave an Indian a gold piece instead of a silver half dollar and he brought it back to my father in a few minutes. Father didn't know what was wrong until he looked at the money. Once there was an Indian man with his squaw and his sister camping on the beach by the store. He proceeded to get drunk. The mosquitoes were about

26. Tebeau, *Chokoloskee Bay Country*, p. 55.

as bad as they ever get but the squaws tied him up and he rolled around on the shell beach all night. Next morning he was still tied up. I have heard the drunken Indians rattle the door knob on our front door and want my father to get up and help them hunt their liquor.

They also came to him for medicine when they were sick. He knew their language and customs and they trusted him. In the 1918 epidemic influenza spread to the Indians at the head of Turner River. Many of them were dying with it. Their medical lore provided no remedy for this new disease. They were said to pour cold water on the feverish ones to cool them.

John Jumper came down with the flu while he was camping on the beach near the store. My dad had John and his family, a wife and two kids, stay in an old house back on the hill about two hundred yards from the store where he could care for the sick man. When his wife wanted my father to give him some medicine she would come down to the store and say "John, John" the only English words she knew. The Indian recovered from the flu and went back into the glades. For a long time he would not come by this side of the island, but would go around the island on the other side.

The Indian women almost never spoke to White people, but they would speak to my father in their own language when they came to trade. If he was not in the store they would point to what they wanted and pay for it an item at a time, Indian fashion.

To the store the Indians brought mostly alligator hides and other skins. Father's account books show that in 1914, for example he was buying alligator hides from Miami Billy, Little Jim Dixie, Little Charlie Jumper, Little Boy Jim, Jim Tiger, Charlie Billy, Charlie Doctor and Jack Osceola. The way the account is kept shows he might have been advancing them supplies and crediting them with the hides they brought in. Seven foot hides are marked at from ninety cents to a dollar apiece.

Indians kept the islanders supplied with fresh venison and wild turkeys. Sometimes they tanned deer hides and brought in the buckskin. In season they might bring in such wild fruits as huckleberries. Billy Jim used to sit at his camp near the shore on the beach and carve small canoes of wood, charging from twenty-five cents to a dollar depending on the size.

Father sold to the Indians hand sewing machines, sewing thread and needles, yards of calico, phonographs and records and accordions. For food he sold them mostly sugar, flour and grits. Their principal item of food was sofkee which they liked to make from coarse grits and cook for hours. Formerly they had grown their own corn and prepared it with mortar and pestle to make the sofkee. When we first knew them they would often roast garfish or turtles or bear meat at their camp fires, but more and more as time went on they bought grits and boiled the sofkee.

This Indian trade came to an end in the nineteen twenties when the Tamiami Trail was completed. This road changed the Indian way of living a great deal and he went elsewhere for markets.

Some of the Indians that came here before the Tamiami Trail went through were: Dr. Tiger and squaw Annie Tiger, Charlie Tigertail, Ingram Billy, Josie Billy, Billy Connapatchee, Abraham Lincoln, Brown Tiger, Little Tiger, Lucie Tiger, John Jumper, Jack Buster, also Young Jack Buster, Frank Willie, Jimmie Willie, Charlie Tommy, Little Charlie Jumper, Chief Charlie Jumper, Tommy Osceola, Dixie and Charlie Cypress.

Abraham Lincoln was helping my father put the foundation under the store when he raised it off the ground in 1925. He quit and told my father that "Think so Smallwood big sleep when I come back" too much heavy work. I don't think he liked to handle those big puncheons very much.[27]

In addition to the colorful recollections of the Smallwood children, the Smallwood store still holds a set of ledgers dating from 1926 (earlier records having been lost in the hurricane that inundated the store) which provide perhaps the most complete set of data on prices during the declining years of the Indian trade in Florida.

W. D. Roberts' family came to the settlement of Immokalee—still a raw frontier town frequented primarily by cattlemen, farmers, and Indians—in 1914 when he was twelve years old.[28] He well remembers the old trader W. H. "Bill" Brown, who was still running his store at that time. All of his life Roberts had contact with the Seminole people, and in 1932 he opened a general store in Immok-

27. Ibid., pp. 56–59.
28. Interview with W. D. Roberts, Immokalee, Aug. 13, 1972. Tape and transcript in University of Florida Indian Oral History Archives, Florida State Museum, Gainesville.

alee where they came to buy groceries and also to trade their hides and furs. A man of high religious conviction, Roberts also sought through his Southern Baptist church to get a mission established for the Indians in the Big Cypress region. Working with Willie King, the Indian missionary from Oklahoma, and later with the dynamic and controversial Indian preacher Stanley Smith, Roberts was instrumental in getting the first Baptist church built on the Big Cypress Reservation; in 1972 he was again actively engaged in the building of a modern structure to house that congregation.

The store which W. D. Roberts opened in November 1932 was nothing more or less than a general store, but it also provided the closest outlet for Indians living on the federal reservation. He bought their alligators, 'coon and otter pelts, buckskins, and other items. The fur was graded and brought from 10¢ to $2.50 for 'coons, while otter ranged from four to ten dollars; however, he recalls the time when an otter brought twenty-five dollars across the board at the end of World War I when things were scarce. At the same time, 'coon skins brought five dollars—they were becoming popular for coats—and the buyer just counted the number of tails in a stack and paid accordingly. Alligator hides brought $1.25 to $1.50 on a clean seven-foot skin with "no buttons—thin bone in the skin that could not be eliminated in the tanning."[29] Roberts shipped his alligator hides to a firm in New Orleans and to Southern Hide & Skins in Jacksonville, which also bought furs. He received a quoted price per grade of hide or skin from the buyers and used this as the basis for setting his own price to the Indians and other hunters; sometimes he had to pay more than he knew he could make on a hide, but he claimed "I never let anybody take the Indian hides away from my place."[30] His main competition at that time came from traveling hide buyers, for there were no other firms in the area buying Indian products. He continued to run the store for fourteen years, selling it after World War II to devote full time to a prosperous ranching enterprise.

Roberts recalls the buying habits of the Indian people who frequented his store: "They always bought what we call staple goods . . . coarse grits which they made sofkee out of . . . meats and some lard, stuff like that that the average country man lived on at that

29. Ibid.
30. Ibid.

time."[31] He always paid the Indians cash, and they were free to buy anywhere they pleased. The Indians bought one article at a time and paid for it so they would know just how much the merchant was charging; later, after they trusted the storekeeper, they became accustomed to "bunching" their purchases. Roberts knew enough of their language to get just about anything an Indian wanted to order without much difficulty. During prohibition he recalls playing a trick on one of the Seminole men who had taken to drinking rubbing alcohol as a substitute for liquor: "I went back and opened up a case of mineral oil with the same type of bottles and the same color of labels, and hid the rubbing alcohol in the mineral oil case and put it back in the back where they couldn't find it. Well, of course he was always liquored up when he came in to get the rubbing alcohol because he was out of whiskey, and he took a pretty good dose of mineral oil before he realized what he was actually drinking. The next time he came in he would look at that bottle up there and talk to the other Indians about it. They didn't get sore . . . they knew I wasn't supposed to sell them rubbing alcohol on that measure, so they never did ask me for rubbing alcohol again."[32] Roberts was a teetotaler who did not want the Indians to have liquor, particularly since many of them had been killed while under the influence of liquor sold by moonshiners in the region. He worked to have those who were selling the illegal liquor prosecuted and felt that, partially through his efforts, the volume of whiskey coming to the Indians was kept fairly well under control until the end of prohibition.

Roberts' store never handled beads or trinkets, but he did sell parts for the Indians' Model-T Ford cars, and they had become good mechanics. One story has it that a group of Indians got their car stuck in a marl prairie, so they disassembled the whole machine and carried it out piece by piece, then reassembled the car and drove away.

In his lifetime at Immokalee since 1914, W. D. Roberts has known intimately both the Seminole people and some of their best friends: W. H. "Bill" Brown, W. Stanley Hanson, the Brown children, Frank and Rose, the Storters and Smallwoods, and countless other hunters and traders who dealt with them. His great concern for the well-being, both physical and spiritual, of the Indian people is probably

31. Ibid.
32. Ibid.

representative of the uniquely close relationship that existed between the frontier traders and the Seminoles in Florida throughout
the years when both Indians and whites lived in relative isolation.
However, by the late 1930s the volume of trade was negligible, the
social isolation of the Indian had begun to change radically under
the impact of improved transportation and communication with the
outside world, and the peak days of the store–trading post were
gone forever.

8

The Seminole Trade in Perspective

In 1930, one-half century after Clay MacCauley's initial study of the Seminole Indians in Florida for the Smithsonian Institution, the federal government sent Roy Nash to conduct yet another survey of the conditions of the Indian population in the southernmost state.[1] This was the last in a long line of visits, such as those of F. C. Churchill in 1909 and L. D. Creel in 1911, in which "special agents" sought the basis for a permanent solution to the "Indian problem" in Florida. With the rapid drainage and settlement of the state during the first quarter of this century, the Seminoles had increasingly become a source of irritation and embarrassment to land developers and officials who were charged with relocating them from populated areas. Through the efforts of groups such as the Friends of the Florida Seminoles, the legislature had established a state Indian reservation of some 99,000 acres in 1917, and the U.S. Indian Service opened the small Dania Reservation in 1926; there were also several thousand acres of federal land in the Big Cypress held in trust for the Seminole people. Nevertheless, at the time of Nash's visit, only a handful of Indians had moved onto the designated reservation lands. Most still clung to their isolated camps on and near the old hunting grounds of the Everglades region; a few lived on the land of farmers for whom they worked, while others found temporary employment and lodging at commercial tourist camps in Miami, Fort Myers, and other cities. In effect, what Nash saw and described in his report to the U.S. Senate was an uprooted and dis-

1. Roy Nash, "Survey of the Seminole Indians of Florida."

possessed people in the nascent stage of socioeconomic transition from a subsistence farming and hunting-trapping economy to an agricultural-herding economy based on their own land.

The Seminole was initially portrayed as a cultural anachronism whose lifestyle, though existing within a few miles of modern metropolitan Miami, had undergone relatively little change in the intervening fifty years since MacCauley's visit. Yet, in his narrative Nash consistently contrasted the old and the new in Seminole life. If the Indian men still wore the colorful long shirt of the last century at times, they also accepted the long trousers of the white man; most males spoke at least some English, and only one man was known to wear his hair in the mode described in 1880. As for the women, their skirts had become even more colorful due mainly to the spread of the sewing machine and the availability of ready-made appliques; a cape had been added to their costume, alleviating the embarrassment formerly afforded by an extended bare midriff, while colorful strands of beads remained their favorite adornment. The Seminole camp with its thatched-roof chickees and wheel-spoke campfire remained essentially unchanged since before the turn of the century, although nails and other materials were now used in construction. Rifles and shotguns had been substituted for the old Kentucky rifles (although this change was under way in the 1890s), the phonograph had become standard camp equipment, while a "second-hand Ford" was accepted along with the family dugout canoe as a means of transportation. On balance, Nash found the Seminoles a very self-sufficient and vigorous people, although unfortunately a bit too addicted to whiskey for their own good, and rapidly approaching an economic crisis in terms of their ability to generate a cash income.

Indeed, for most of the Seminole families it was a time of great privation as they eked out a living in any way possible; a few had already entered into the wage-work economy picking beans, tomatoes, and other field crops in season, and by the end of the decade there would be the beginning of a beef cattle industry on the reservations. Still, many like the family of Whitney Cypress, described in detail by Nash, adhered to the old ways which were fast disappearing. Their basic subsistence came from a small garden of corn, pumpkin, sweet potatoes, sugarcane, and peas, as well as the products of hunting and fishing: venison, turkey, duck, and fish. Of course there was the ever-present sofkee pot which was a mainstay of any Seminole camp. The real difficulty came in securing money with which to buy the groceries and supplies that the Indians had come to depend upon from the trading posts. Nash reported that "the cash income of this family is derived almost entirely from the sale of raccoon and alligator skins, buckskin, and an occasional otter. The women make a few dollars from the sale of Seminole dolls and a little very indifferent bead work. Whitney is an unusually industrious hunter and probably takes in $300 a year from his pelts. In addition, he may get an opportunity to guide hunters for a couple of weeks each fall in the open season, at $6 a day for himself and oxcart, with a bonus of a ten dollar bill and a quart of liquor for killing the buck his employer could not hit."[2] How different from the times when an Indian hunter could bring in hundreds of dollars worth of pelts and hides every few weeks.

Nash undertook a thorough examination of the volume and value of the Indian trade in Florida. He consulted with major dealers such as John J. Fohl of Fort Myers; A. A. Harrington of Arcadia and his partner J. E. Carter at Canal Point; William Poole at LaBelle; R. L. Pierce, Calvin Drawdy, and Nate Zelmenovitz of Okeechobee; Evan Kenzie at Dania; as well as Bert Lasher and Kiser at Miami. From them he learned that "the Indian is a minority factor in the Florida fur trade."[3] Fohl, for example, did some $22,300 worth of trade in hides and skins annually, but only 35 per cent of his business was with the Seminoles. By putting together the estimates of transactions with Indians from each of these dealers, Nash arrived at an approximate value of the Indian trade: $34,000. However, this was not the amount that the Indians actually realized; taking into consideration the fact that some of the furs passed through middlemen (Fohl and Harrington dealt primarily with local men who bought from the Indians), and that the Indian's constant need for cash and desire for liquor often led him to sell for well below market value, Nash felt that a more realistic figure would be $25,000 that the Seminoles actually received.

Yet, prices for pelts and hides had risen as they became more scarce in the Everglades. A raccoon skin brought from thirty-five cents to $2.50; alligator hides varied from twenty-five cents for a three-foot tanned hide to three dollars for a seven-footer; otter brought twelve to fifteen dollars each. All of these prices were sig-

2. Ibid., p. 10.
3. Ibid., p. 36.

nificantly higher than those reported by L. D. Creel in his 1911 report. What's more, the volume of trade had begun to rise in the
prosperous years of the late 1920s prior to the stock market crash.
At Fort Myers, Fohl was handling 5,000 raccoon skins and 10,000
alligator hides, along with 400 otter hides per year. The problem
was that the Seminoles could no longer successfully compete with
the white hunter for the game that was left. As Nash put it, "Although hunting is the Seminole's chief industry, he is regularly
beaten at his own game by white men. Zane Grey tells of meeting
an Indian on Broad River who had killed 11 alligators the night
before using a torch. Alphonso Lopez, of Everglades . . . said that
he and his brother in a lake at Cape Sable killed 103 in two nights,
using a powerful reflector. It is the difference between a dugout
canoe and a gasoline launch. Lopez also told me that he and his
brother will average 500 skins each, mostly raccoon, in two months
trapping on the Monroe County Reservation. White men buy better
traps and take more pains in handling their pelts."[4]

Although the lucrative era of the Indian trade came to an end
during the late 1920s, it had been on the decline since the turn of
the century. The decision to drain the Everglades sealed the fate
of that region insofar as hunting the alligator and otter was con-
cerned. As early as 1908, W. H. "Bill" Brown predicted the demise
of the 'gator trade which was the mainstay of the "Boat Landing"
and sought a more permanent location back in Immokalee. In 1912
the Commissioner of Indian Affairs reported to Senator Duncan U.
Fletcher that "during the past year the tanneries have stopped the
purchase of alligator skins, so that now a crisis is approaching, as
at least 75 per cent of the Indian's income was derived from that
source."[5] Two years later, Dr. W. J. Godden, who had succeeded
Bill Brown at the "Boat Landing" under the auspices of the Episcopal Church, found that the Indian trade had diminished to a point
where they were in great need, and he embarked upon the Seminole
farm project. His report spurred the Seminole Indian Association, a
group organized by W. Stanley Hanson of Fort Myers, to appeal
urgently to the federal government for relief funds for the Indians
living in the Big Cypress.[6] The market for alligator hides had been

4. Ibid., p. 37–38.
5. U.S., Congress, Senate, *Seminole Indians in Florida*, Senate Doc. 42, 63d
Cong., 1st sess., 1913, p. 5.
6. *Fort Myers Daily Press*, Sept. 22, 1914, p. 3.

generally poor after 1898 due to overhunting, the importation of the South American cayman, and ultimately the drainage programs; the loss of European markets with the outbreak of World War I severely crippled the Seminole trade, and it never recovered. By 1921, Indian Agent L. A. Spencer reported that "the year just closing has been a season of distress for many of the Seminoles. There was no demand for fur or alligator hides, the only two things that they depend on to obtain money with which to buy the necessities of life other than those which they obtain through hunting."[7] It was continuing reports such as these which led to the Nash Survey of 1930 and its sweeping recommendations for dealing with the Florida Indians.

Essentially, Nash recommended that the Indian service should continue to function among the Seminoles in Florida for the next quarter century, but that the service should also survey the situation at least every decade to see how conditions had changed and what services were needed. In the meantime, he wisely suggested that "title to no land be alienated by allotments or otherwise."[8] By following this course, the reservation lands would remain intact for the day when they could be developed as a tribal enterprise benefiting all of the Seminole people. A man of vigorous physique should be employed as the Seminole agent, one who would spend his time getting to know the Indians and gaining their trust, for "the Seminole can be led by one he trusts, but cannot be driven."[9] Due to the rugged terrain that he would have to traverse and the multiplicity of duties he would be called upon to perform, Nash ventured that "if the agent did not use up one Ford car a year, I should suspect him of neglecting his work."[10] He suggested the continuation of the Indian Day School at Dania, but would keep it an elementary school and transfer the Indian youngsters into public schools as soon as possible. Similarly, health services were to be upgraded through the use of contract doctors and dentists and a visiting Public Health nurse in the camps; however, hospitalization should be limited to public hospitals, preferably in Miami. In general, Nash tended to prefer integrating Seminole educational and health services into

7. U.S., Congress, Senate, *Special Report of the Florida Seminole Agency,* Senate Doc. 102, 67th Cong., 2d sess., 1921, p. 5.
8. Nash, "Survey of the Seminole Indians of Florida," p. 83.
9. Ibid.
10. Ibid., p. 85.

existing South Florida programs rather than erecting parallel programs for Indians alone.

As for economic development, Nash held that the great hope for the future lay not in farming but in the development of a beef cattle industry among the Indians, noting that "it seems to me that we, the representatives of the civilization which drove the Seminole out of the cattle business, have got to start at the very beginning and remake him into a cattleman. . . . Buy a few head of ordinary Florida range cattle, which can be had on occasion at less than $20 a head, buy a beef-type bull, and let him begin to build a Government herd. The Cypress Indians will probably look the first year or two. Then some of the boys will learn to ride and use a rope. Take them into Government employ as the herd increases. In the course of years some will surely develop enough business sense so that cattle can safely be sold to them on terms they can meet."[11] In an uncanny way, Nash had predicted almost exactly how the Seminole cattle industry would develop over the next four decades.

Although he did not totally discount the continuation of hunting and trapping for some time, and in fact assumed it would provide a supplementary income while the agricultural enterprises were developed, Nash nevertheless cautioned against counting on it indefinitely. Even so, hunting and trapping still accounted for 66 per cent of the Seminole cash income, the remainder being derived from such things as the sale of dresses, dolls, beads, buckskin items, and huckleberries, day work as field laborers and hunting guides, as well as from employment in tourist attractions and some outright begging. Inevitably, factors were combining to eventually force the Indian totally out of the hunting-trapping economy. Perhaps most important was the state imposition of an open hunting season on fur-bearing animals that was only from December to March; anything the Seminole took after that was illegal poaching, and this included the venison and turkey that were hunted both for food and profit. That left only alligators as a year-round source of income, but they were becoming scarce and the Indian was in competition with better equipped white hunters, as noted before. Moreover, at that time the proposal that would ultimately eventuate in Everglades National Park had been made, and that could only lead to a further diminution of Indian hunting grounds. Thus, even though Nash proposed that a trading post be established on the Hendry County

11. Ibid., p. 79.

reservation, he had effectively written the obituary of the Seminole trade in pelts, plumes, and hides.

When reconstructing the years of the Seminole trade in Florida, one is taken with the fact that the major drama was played out in something less than a half-century, as opposed to the western Indian trade that lasted for most of the nation's history from the Revolutionary War until the tribes were finally conquered near the end of the nineteenth century.[12] Certainly this was due in part to Florida's unique position as one of the last frontiers to be settled, its abundance of marketable wildlife quickly exploited and land rapidly taken up by agricultural interests or sold to northerners seeking the promise of an easier life in the mild climate. Thus, the southern portion of the peninsula progressed from raw frontier to a well-settled area in a relatively short time, due to the railroads of Flagler and Plant which provided Florida growers access to northern markets and brought in hordes of tourists. The promotional literature of land development companies and an interesting body of Floridiana by prominent literary figures such as Harriet Beecher Stowe, Sidney Lanier, Kirk Munroe, and others, also captured the imagination of the nation and projected the state as the nearest thing to a tropical Eden on this continent. Nevertheless, in the decades of the 1880s and '90s, it was the lure of profit from plumes, pelts, and hides which primarily attracted men like Storter, Brown, and Stranahan to the wilds of South Florida, and in the beginning the Seminoles were their main suppliers.

As the Seminoles hunted and trapped the Everglades in a circuit of some three hundred miles between Lake Okeechobee and the Ten Thousand Islands, they could trade with any number of "whiskey men" who came into the hunting grounds with groceries and liquor; later the permanent trading posts established along the periphery of the 'glades offered an outlet for their products, as well as more stable prices and the possibility of some credit in bad times. For the first twenty years of the heavy trading period, the Indians were the dominant factor, but by the 1890s increasing numbers of professional white hunters had arrived in the region. They were generally better armed, well organized (especially the plume hunters, who could

12. For representative views of the Indian trade in the United States see Frank McNitt, *The Indian Traders*; Robert G. Atherton, *Forts of the Upper Missouri*; Henry A. Boller, *Among the Indians: Four Years on the Upper Missouri, 1858–1862*, ed. M. M. Quaife; Gen. Thomas James, *Three Years among the Indians and Mexicans*, ed. M. M. Quaife.

systematically exterminate a rookery in a day or two), and, as a group, quite ruthless in their wanton destruction of the game. The Indians, on the other hand, hunted not so much for profit as to sustain life either by consuming their catch or selling its pelt to buy items needed for survival; they rarely overkilled the game and always retained a respect for the delicate balance of the natural environment. As a result, the Seminoles never reaped the huge profits realized by white hunters. By the late 1880s the demand for plumes used in women's fashions led to rapid exhaustion of rookeries in the Kissimmee River and Caloosahatchee River valleys. In 1892 one agent reportedly shipped 130,000 birds from Florida, and this number rose to 192,000 a decade later; with an ounce of feathers bringing up to $32, the millinery industry in New York was reportedly doing a $17 million business by the time of the antipluming law in 1910.[13] Although the Seminoles had brought in egret and curlew plumes to trade, they were rarely superordinate in that market, either in terms of money (Ewan at Miami was paying twenty-five cents each for plumes in the '70s, while Storter and Brown offered only fifty to seventy-five cents at the turn of the century) or volume, compared to the whites.

As early as the 1880s the trade in alligator hides was brisk in Florida, with as many as 50,000 hides being shipped annually; one trapper reportedly contracted to deliver 5,000 to a single Paris leather firm.[14] A decade later, traders like Storter at Everglade and Bill Brown at his "Boat Landing" in the Big Cypress were taking in as many as 5,000 hides each month. Although white hunters took their share of alligators by employing miners' lanterns, power launches, and high-powered rifles to hunt the saurian at night, it was the Seminoles working the backwaters of the Everglades who provided most of the 'gator hides prior to World War I. When their trade prospered, many Indians adopted the white man's mode of hunting, as graphically described by A. W. Dimock and Kirk Munroe,[15] thereby further increasing their income. Unfortunately, from around the turn of the century the hide market was highly volatile, and the traders never knew exactly what, if anything, they would receive from green salted hides at the tanneries. The Sem-

13. Hanna and Hanna, *Lake Okeechobee*, pp. 341–42. See also Charles M. Brookfield and Oliver Griswold, *They All Called It Tropical*, pp. 69–72.
14. Ibid., p. 343.
15. Kirk Munroe, "Alligator Hunting with Seminoles," pp. 576–81. A. W. Dimock and Julian A. Dimock, *Florida Enchantments*, pp. 116-20.

inoles realized good money from otter pelts, but otter also became scarce after the Everglades water table was lowered. Raccoon skins rose in value during the "roaring 20s," but the Seminoles reportedly disdained trapping the animals due to their odor, and this might account for some of their lack of success in exploiting the market when it returned. Even so, the ingenuity and better equipment of the white trapper apparently were the decisive factors in reducing the Seminoles to an inferior position by the time of Nash's visit.

The pattern of interaction differed very little among the trading posts. The Seminoles traded at the store most convenient to the area in which they were hunting and expected to receive essentially the same price for their goods. This mobility of the Indian is borne out by the same names appearing on different account books and in the reminiscences of traders throughout the region; a few, of course, like those with camps near Fort Lauderdale or Everglade did most of their trading with one store through much of the year. The traders apparently formed what economists might call an "oligopoly" which set prices in a given trading area. Moreover, this very stability of prices regardless of the national market was (as shall be seen) an essential element in trading with Indians. On the other hand, the Indians did not seem to be aware of any difference in prices charged them and the white settlers—if indeed there was any difference. On the whole, the Seminoles appeared satisfied in their economic and social relationships with the great majority of the trading families.

The cash flow at the trading posts appears to have been restricted, due to the Indian practice of receiving money for their trade items, then making purchases in the stores an item at a time. Evidently the storekeepers kept little cash money on hand, for they received back practically all that was paid out on a given day. It is interesting to conjecture what might have happened if a significant number of Indians had begun keeping their money rather than spending it before leaving the store, especially at isolated posts like Everglade and "Boat Landing" which were days from the nearest banking institutions. It is possible that this would have forced the trader to curtail the number of pelts and hides that he accepted, thereby creating an economic and public relations problem of the first magnitude. Generally, the Indians came in to trade only when they needed supplies, so this type of confrontation apparently never occurred. Furthermore, the Seminoles depended upon the traders for credit in times when hunting had been poor. For example, it is known that

Storter allowed them to "make book," while Smallwood granted credit against future catches of alligator hides and otter. At Stranahan & Company a special Indian credit ledger was maintained, and it is from this document and accompanying sales slips that we are able to piece together a picture of how one trader dealt with the Seminoles.

A recent study of the Stranahan & Company ledgers for 1906–12 by Professor J. C. Nicholas reveals some unique facets of the Seminole trade early in this century.[16] Over that period, the retail prices which Stranahan charged to Indians averaged 140 per cent of those charged to whites. At first glance such a difference would appear to be highly discriminatory and therefore consistent with previous studies of Indian-white trade relationships. However, it would not have been consistent with Stranahan's reputation for honesty and fair dealing with the Indian people. Numerous sources have vouched for his character, and observers such as Nash counted him among the staunchest friends of the Florida Seminoles; moreover, one of the tribe accorded him the ultimate compliment by adopting the name Little Stranahan. If the Indians had suspected that he was not dealing fairly with them, there is little doubt that they would have discontinued trading at the store and seeking Stranahan's counsel. Thus, one must look to the very nature of Indian trading habits, along with fluctuations in wholesale prices for hides and pelts, to provide an alternative explanation of price differentiations other than discrimination in this case.

Stranahan traded for both alligator hides and otter pelts, which were the mainstays of the Seminole economy. In turn, he would sell these items at a profit to tanneries and dealers such as Southern Hides and Skins Co. and Osky's, both located in Jacksonville, or John White & Co. in Louisville, Kentucky. The general practice was for Stranahan to take in enough goods to make a shipment, get bids, and ship to the highest bidder. The Florida trader usually established a pattern of selling to certain houses and accepted the price that was currently being quoted, and prices fluctuated rapidly. The important point is that the trader did not have a firm market; he stood to gain a windfall with price increases or to bear a loss during a declining market. There were times when Stranahan could not even get bids for his hides and pelts from his usual buyers, and on

16. James C. Nicholas, "The Economics of the Indian Trade in Florida" (manuscript).

one occasion the price for live baby alligators (a profitable business that he continued to engage in after selling the store) dropped 25 per cent in one week.[17] The character of his trade goods—green salted hides that created a great stench and deteriorated rapidly, and otter pelts that were susceptible to insects and rotting—precluded holding an inventory until market conditions improved. The baby alligators, although they were alive and could be penned, were voracious eaters and soon outgrew their optimum size as tourist souveniers. In addition, Stranahan had to turn over his goods to secure cash with which to purchase supplies for the store. The records of the Stranahan store show that the risks of the Indian trader were great, and this was probably typical of most of the others doing business in Florida at that time.

The Seminoles, however, were unaware of the market price fluctuations for the goods that they brought in to trade and expected a more or less stable price for a commodity such as 'gator hides. It fell to the trader to absorb the price fluctuations or risk the enmity of his Seminole clientele. Stranahan was apparently willing to hold a constant price for 'gator hides during the 1906–12 period, although by the end of that time the market for alligator hides had seriously deteriorated due to factors previously set forth. The way in which he protected himself in this declining market was to raise the prices of the goods sold to Indians to reflect their reduced buying power. Professor Nicholas has conjectured that

> The Indian's insistence upon the use of cash as an intermediary in bartering in addition to his expectation of a fixed price for his goods offered in trade becomes the grounds for the appearance of price discrimination. The decline in wholesale prices for hides resulted in an increase in the hides to goods ratio. In addition, during this time period the prices of goods themselves tended to rise. That further increased the hides to goods ratio. Thus, the expectations of the Indian in conjunction with his mobility led to a situation where it was easier to alter the hides to goods ratio to a new equilibrium point by increasing the price of goods while holding the price of hides constant. The whites who were in the hides and pelts trade as hunters did not deal with Stranahan and therefore all white customers were in the non-bartering category. What the

17. Ibid., p. 10.

trader wanted to avoid was a confrontation with the Indians on prices. . . .

What is suggested here is that the observed price differential between Indian and white buyers has another explanation than simple price discrimination. The Indians of Florida had a deep distrust of the white race in general and distrusted the government most of all. The Indians had only a very rudimentary knowledge of the English language. Thus, even if trust existed between the races the trader really could not communicate the elements of wholesale price fluctuations due to their mutual inabilities to speak the language of the other. The Indian saw the trader as the one who set the prices and felt that his price was universal. If he were to receive less than ten cents per foot, the hunter would stop trading with the person giving him the lower price. If all traders had reduced the price the Indian would most certainly suspected them of cheating him. The Indian's insistence upon payment in cash for hides left the trader no alternative but to adjust for wholesale price movements by adjusting retail prices.[18]

After assessing the evidence found in the Stranahan ledgers, Nicholas contends there is basis to argue that, rather than being discriminated against, the Seminoles were charged prices on a par with white buyers when prices are adjusted to reflect the reduced purchasing power of the alligator hides. This conclusion is strengthened by the fact that the price differential grew during the period, whereas the wholesale price of hides declined. In conclusion, the Nicholas study holds that the economics of the Indian trade in Florida conforms nicely with the law of supply and demand. As increasing supplies of hides were offered, the wholesale prices diminished. The problem arose in passing this price decline back to the Indians. His paper suggests that the secular decline in the wholesale price of alligator hides, and thus, their purchasing power, was passed on to the Indians by means of a readjustment in retail prices.[19]

At this point one can logically raise the question of how typical the Stranahan situation was vis-à-vis the other Indian traders. Enjoying rather easy access to both sea and (after 1896) rail transportation, Frank Stranahan was in a more advantageous position to market his goods than Storter at Everglade or Brown at his "Boat

18. Ibid., pp. 13–14.
19. Ibid., p. 15.

Landing" location. If anything, the other traders were even more dependent on buyers in Fort Myers and Tampa, and took practically any price that was offered for the commodities that they brought in periodically. Unfortunately, no other detailed set of books like the Stranahan Indian ledgers exists for the first quarter of this century; thus any comparisons must be purely conjectural.[20] Nevertheless, the Nicholas study stands as the first attempt to develop a trading model based on the limited data currently available to researchers.

Aside from serving as economic intermediaries for the Seminoles, the traders also exerted great influence on the evolving life style of the Indian people. Their major impact, of course, was in providing a catalyst for the Seminole shift from a subsistence to a market economy in which they became more dependent on the white man's goods. Through their frequent contacts with the families residing at the trading posts, the Indians learned to use a great many articles through imitation, but in some cases they also received instruction from the whites. Probably the most notable introduction of new technology into Seminole culture in this manner was the hand-cranked sewing machine which came into general use during the 1880s. It will be recalled that at the time of MacCauley's visit, the Seminoles were wearing clothing made of "calico, cotton, ginghams, and sometimes flannels,"[21] but there was no evidence of anything other than handsewn garments. However, Goggin has reported that there was one sewing machine among the Seminoles in 1880,[22] Dr. Brecht recorded their general use in his reports during the 1890s,[23] while

20. By all odds, the Stranahan ledgers are the most pertinent set of records dealing with the Seminole trade in Florida. Only three other ledgers exist from the early trading period: the ledger from L. M. Raulerson in Okeechobee beginning in 1917, a fragment of the Brickell ledgers from the 1890s, and the Smallwood Store ledgers at Chokoloskee. The Brickell and Raulerson ledgers make little distinction between prices charged to Indians and other customers and therefore are useless for the type of comparative analysis attempted by Dr. Nicholas. The Smallwood books from 1926 onward are a potential bonanza of information on the declining years of the Seminole trade in southwest Florida, but the family has not opened them to scholarly research.

21. Clay MacCauley, "The Seminole Indians of Florida," p. 483.

22. John M. Goggin, "Florida's Indians," p. 3.

23. U.S., Congress, House, *Report of the Commissioner of Indian Affairs*, Exec. Doc. 1, 53d Cong., 2d sess., 1893, p. 357. Dr. Brecht reported that the Seminole women "sew quite well, and a few machines are now found among the camps." In the same report he decried the role of the traders and whiskey sellers in keeping the Indians away from the mission and government station at Immokalee, claiming "I found the Indians scattered and intensely shy, and greatly troubled in consequence of the malicious work of traders and

Davis' study of changing Seminole clothing notes that "shortly before the turn of the century the Seminole women began to buy the hand-operated machines at the trading posts. It was not long after this that the styles of both the men's and women's clothing began to show decided changes."[24]

It is interesting that practically none of the writers who have discussed Seminole clothing in relation to the sewing machine ever raised the question of how the Indians learned to use it. Certainly a complex piece of machinery that involves at least a modicum of instruction for proper use even today did not automatically become useful to the Indians of the Everglades and Big Cypress. Both Mrs. Stranahan at Fort Lauderdale and Mrs. Brown at the "Boat Landing" are known to have taught Seminole women, as well as a number of men, to use the Singer and White models sold in their husbands' stores, and it is most likely that a similar process took place at other trading posts as the machines became available. Later on, storekeepers such as Girtman began to carry readymade items like bias fold, edging, and rick-rack for the Seminole seamstresses to use in making their designs. Thus, Seminole clothing, perhaps the most distinguishing feature of their material culture to this day, evolved over a long period of time with the aid of the traders and their families.

Another area in which the trading families facilitated the acculturation of the Seminoles was education. The work of Mrs. Stranahan in teaching Indian youngsters the three R's and later in founding an organization for the purpose of fostering Seminole schooling, is well documented and needs no further comment. So, too, did Mrs. W. H. Brown spend some time in teaching Indian adults the rudiments of reading and writing; and the missionary-storekeeper Dr. W. J. Godden made attempts along the same line. Although it would be too strong to suggest that the traders paved the way for Seminole acceptance of schooling (perhaps with the exception of Mrs. Stranahan in the special situation that prevailed in her area) at a later time, at least their interest in teaching the Indians such skills was evidence that their aims were not purely mer-

---

others, who realized that an uplifting of these Indians would cut off their nefarious gain, etc." It is not clear, however, whether he was alluding to all traders or just those who frequented the Seminole camps and traded liquor for pelts and hides.

24. Hilda J. Davis, "The History of Seminole Clothing and Its Multi-Colored Designs," p. 975.

cenary. In this same vein, the trading families were often called upon to minister to sick and injured Indians who sought aid at the trading posts. Apparently there was little reluctance on the part of the Seminoles to accept assistance from whites when their own tribal medicine men were either unavailable or unable to help effect a cure. The greatest impact of both Dr. Brecht at Immokalee and Dr. Godden at Glades Cross and later at the "Boat Landing" hospital, was in helping sick Indians—especially in times of epidemics such as measles and influenza, which took a dreadful toll. Likewise, the Browns, Storters, and Smallwoods are known to have assisted the Seminoles during similar outbreaks of communicable diseases. The net result of these efforts to be a "good friend" to the Seminoles in times of need was a residual of good will that transcended a mere economic relationship. A genuine affection often existed between the trading families and many of their Seminole customers; the reminiscences of the families in the preceding chapters bear this out eloquently. The Seminoles and traders, particularly their children, learned to love and share the beauty of the South Florida wilderness by camping, hunting, and trapping together, and rarely was there a festive occasion at the frontier settlements from Chokoloskee to Fort Pierce that did not include the local Seminole contingent— though few events rivaled the Christmas barbecue by "Bill" Brown at "Boat Landing."

All in all, the great lesson to be learned from these narratives is that two totally different cultures could peacefully coexist in the same environment, drawing from and adding to the other, in a symbiotic existence. For what the trader gave in terms of formal education and treatment of disease or as an outlet for goods, he received the Seminole knowledge of herbal medicine, uses of the products of the Everglades, and a constant flow of profitable pelts, plumes, and hides. To the extent that the Seminole displayed such cultural anachronisms—perhaps borrowed would be a more appropriate term—as the derby hat, conductor's cap, and gold watch chains with fobs as part of their garb, so, too, the white man learned to pole a dugout canoe, thatch a chickee roof for shelter, and spice his English with Creek and Mikasuki terms that became common frontier idioms. When, by the 1930s, observers such as Nash found the Ford automobile a part of a traditional chickee camp, or the hand-cranked sewing machine used alongside the sofkee pot, whose origin is lost in antiquity, they were but observing the next to last step in an evolutionary process that had been going on since the Spanish and English colonists made their first trading contacts with the southeastern Indians three centuries ago. The dynamic interaction during the great period of Indian trading in Florida between 1870 and 1930 only accelerated this process of acculturation, with the Seminoles selectively adopting those elements of the dominant culture which were compatible with their traditional values and life style. In the terminology of cultural anthropologist Ralph Linton, they had only changed those specialties of their culture which could be accommodated by their core of universal values, thereby regulating the amount and direction of change in the society.[25] However, when this core of Seminole values began to give way in succeeding decades under the impact of Christianity and the destructive forces attendant to rapid settlement of South Florida, the rate of acculturation increased alarmingly and threatened to obliterate all vestiges of Seminole culture as the trading families had known it at the turn of the century.

The Florida "land boom" of the 1920s signaled the beginning of the end for the traditional Seminole way of life. With the completion of the Tamiami Trail in 1928, linking the lower east coast with the west coast of the state, plus the addition of secondary roads throughout the region, the Indians had easier access to coastal towns and cities for shopping and employment. Unfortunately, this also brought them into closer contact with the baser elements of the dominant culture, and many Indian families were ensnared in the vicious life of the commercial tourist camps which sprang up during that period. But few Seminoles willingly chose to move into the populated urban areas for any length of time; they began to acquire cars and trucks and were frequent visitors, but preferred to keep their camps in wilderness seclusion. As the Everglades were inexorably drained and the game played out, increasing numbers of Indians turned to some form of agricultural pursuit, and the thought of taking up federal lands held in trust for them became an attractive alternative to squatting on someone else's land or living as tenants on the farms where they worked. By the late 1930s, nearly a majority of the tribe had moved on to the reservation lands.

In the long run, perhaps the single most important factor in securing the economic future of the Seminoles was the establishment of these federal reservations in Florida. With land of their own and

25. Ralph Linton, *The Study of Man*, pp. 272–87.

federal economic and technical support, the tribe took to cattle raising and agricultural labor, as well as semi-skilled and skilled construction work both on and off the reservations; their children began to attend school; modern housing supplanted the chickee; and a new life style began to emerge.[26] Today, the Seminoles rarely hunt or trap except for recreation, and stringent game laws govern those activities except on reservation lands. The Miccosukee tribe, which lives along the Tamiami Trail and maintains the most traditional cultural pattern among the Florida Indians, did a thriving business as late as the 1950s supplying restaurants in Miami and the Everglades City–Naples area with frogs' legs and other delicacies.[27] Now even the Miccosukee have turned to commercial ventures with the establishment of a tribal restaurant–service station complex at Forty Mile Bend on the Tamiami Trial west of Miami. Thus, for all practical purposes, the days of commercial hunting and trapping are over for the Indians in Florida; in the not-too-distant future the young Indian will probably look on the hunting and trading period of his people's history as a quaint cultural anachronism, better left to the studies of anthropologists and historians while the Seminole and Miccosukee people get on with the serious business of life in the twentieth century.

26. For information on Seminole educational development see Harry A. Kersey, Jr., "Educating the Seminole Indians of Florida, 1879–1970," and Kersey, "The Ahfachkee Day School."

27. Ethel Cutler Freeman, "Culture Stability and Change among the Seminoles of Florida," *Men and Cultures*, p. 251. For an account of how one Seminole girl made the transition from a frog hunter's chickee to higher education see Merwyn S. Garbarino, "Seminole Girl," pp 40–46. By the 1960s frog hunting was no longer important as a source of income for those Seminoles who had moved on to the Big Cypress reservation; see Garbarino, *Big Cypress, A Changing Seminole Community*, p. 22.

Bibliography

BOOKS

Andrews, Allen H. *A Yank Pioneer in Florida.* Jacksonville, 1950.
Atherton, Robert G. *Forts of the Upper Missouri.* Lincoln, Neb., 1967.
Bell, Emily Lagow. *My Pioneer Days in Florida, 1876–1898.* Miami, 1928.
Bemrose, John. *Reminiscences of the Second Seminole War.* Edited by John K. Mahon. Gainesville, 1966.
Blassingame, Wyatt. *Seminoles of Florida.* Tallahassee, 1959.
Boller, Henry A. *Among the Indians: Four Years on the Upper Missouri, 1858–1862.* Edited by M. M. Quaife. Lincoln, Neb., 1972.
Boyd, Mark F., Smith, Hale G., and Griffin, John W. *Here They Once Stood.* Gainesville, 1951.
Brookfield, Charles M., and Griswold, Oliver. *They All Called It Tropical.* Miami, 1949.
Burghard, August. *Watchie-Esta/Hutrie (The Little White Mother).* Fort Lauderdale, 1968.
Cash, W. T. *The Story of Florida.* 4 vols. New York, 1938.
Coe, Charles H. *Red Patriots: The Story of the Seminoles.* Cincinnati, 1898.
Cohen, Isidor. *Historical Sketches and Sidelights of Miami, Fla.* Cambridge, Mass., 1925. (This book was privately printed.)
Cohen, M. M. *Notices of Florida and the Campaigns.* Reprinted with an introduction by O. Z. Tyler, Jr., in the Floridiana Facsimile and Reprint Series, University of Florida Press. Gainesville, 1964.
Cory, Charles B. *Hunting and Fishing in Florida.* Boston, 1896.
Dimock, A. W., and Dimock, Julian A. *Florida Enchantments.* New York, 1908.
Dovell, Junius E. *Florida, Historic, Dramatic, Contemporary.* 4 vols. New York, 1952.
Federal Writer's Project of the Work Projects Administration. *The Seminole Indians in Florida.* Tallahassee, 1951.
Foreman, Grant. *The Five Civilized Tribes.* Norman, Okla., 1934.
———. *Indian Removal.* Norman, Okla., 1932.
Frazure, Hoyt. *Memories of Old Miami.* Miami, 1969.
Fritz, Florence. *Unknown Florida.* Miami, 1963.

Garbarino, Merwyn S. *Big Cypress, A Changing Seminole Community*. New York, 1972.

Gatewood, George W. *Ox Cart Days to Airplane Era in Southwest Florida*. Fort Myers, 1944.

Gifford, John C. *Billy Bowlegs and the Seminole War*. Coconut Grove, Fla., 1925.

Goggin, John M. *Indian and Spanish Selected Writings*. Edited by C. H. Fairbanks, Irving Rouse, and W. C. Sturtevant. Miami. 1964.

Hanna, Alfred J., and Hanna, Kathryn A. *Lake Okeechobee*. New York, 1948.

Hartley, William, and Hartley, Ellen. *A Woman Set Apart*. New York, 1963.

Hellier, Walter R. *Indian River, Florida's Treasure Coast*. Coconut Grove, Fla., 1965.

Henshall, James A. *Camping and Cruising in Florida*. Cincinnati, 1884.

Jackson, Helen Hunt. *A Century of Dishonor*. New York, 1881.

James, Gen. Thomas. *Three Years among the Indians and Mexicans*. Edited by M. M. Quaife. New York, 1966.

Levitan, Sar A., and Hetrick, Barbara. *Big Brother's Indian Programs—with Reservations*. New York, 1971.

Linton, Ralph. *The Study of Man*. New York, 1936.

Lyons, Ernest. *My Florida*. New York, 1969.

Mahon, John K. *History of the Second Seminole War, 1835–1842*. Gainesville, 1967.

Manypenny, G. W. *Our Indian Wards*. New York, 1879.

McGoun, Bill. *A Biographic History of Broward County*. Miami, 1972.

McKay, D. B. *Pioneer Florida*. 3 vols. Tampa, 1959.

McNitt, Frank. *The Indian Traders*. Norman, Okla., 1962.

McReynolds, Edwin C. *The Seminoles*. Norman, Okla., 1957.

Moore-Willson, Minnie. *The Seminoles of Florida*. New York, 1896.

Muir, Helen. *Miami, U.S.A.* Coconut Grove, Fla., 1953.

Munroe, Ralph Middleton, and Gilpin, Vincent. *The Commodore's Story*. Narbeth, Pa., 1966.

Nance, E. C., ed. *The East Coast of Florida*. 3 vols. Delray Beach, Fla., 1962.

Neill, Wilfred T. *Florida's Seminole Indians*. Silver Springs, Fla., 1952.

Parkhill, Harriet Randolph. *Mission to the Seminoles*. Orlando, 1909.

Pearse, Eleanor H. D. *Florida's Vanishing Era*. Privately published, 1954.

Peithman, Irving M. *The Unconquered Seminole Indians*. St. Petersburg, 1957.

Pierce, Charles W. *Pioneer Life in Southeast Florida*. Edited by Donald W. Curl. Miami, 1970.

Pizzo, Anthony P. *Tampa Town*. Miami, 1968.

Pratt, Richard H. *Battlefield and Classroom*. Edited by Robert Utley. New Haven, 1964.

Robertson, William B., Jr. *Everglades—The Park Story*. Miami, 1959.

Robertson, W. S. and Winslett, David. *Muskogee or Creek First Reader*. Okmulgee, Okla., 1963. Reprint of original by Presbyterian Board of Christian Education, Philadelphia, Pa.

Sprague, John T. *The Origin, Progress, and Conclusion of the Florida War*. New York, 1848. Reprinted with an introduction by John K. Mahon in the Floridiana Facsimile and Reprint Series, University of Florida Press. Gainesville, 1964.

Storter, R. L. *Seventy-Seven Years at Everglades, Chokoloskee, Naples*. Naples, Fla., 1972.

Stuart, Hix G. *The Notorious Ashley Gang*. Stuart, Fla., 1928.

Tebeau, Charlton W. *Florida's Last Frontier*. Miami, 1966.

————. *Man in the Everglades*. Miami, 1968.
————. *The Story of the Chokoloskee Bay Country*. Miami, 1955.
Weidling, Philip, and Burghard, August. *Checkered Sunshine, the History of Fort Lauderdale 1793–1955*. Gainesville, 1966.
Will, Lawrence E. *A Cracker History of Okeechobee*. St. Petersburg, 1964.
Willoughby, Hough L. *Across the Everglades*. Philadelphia, 1896.

ARTICLES AND REPORTS

Bentley, George R. "Colonel Thompson's Tour of Tropical Florida." *Tequesta* 10 (1950):3–12.
Capron, Louis. "Florida's Emerging Seminoles." *National Geographic* 126 (1969):716–34.
————. "Florida's 'Wild' Indians, The Seminoles." *National Geographic* 90 (1956):819–40.
————. "The Medicine Bundles of the Florida Seminole and the Green Corn Dance." Smithsonian Institution, Bureau of American Ethnology, Bulletin 51. Washington, 1953.
————. "Notes on the Hunting Dance of the Cow Creek Seminole." *Florida Anthropologist* 9 (1956):67–78.
Church, Alonzo. "A Dash through the Everglades." *Tequesta* 9 (1949):15–41.
Conrad, Mary Douthit. "Homesteading in Florida during the 1890's." *Tequesta* 17 (1957):1–15.
Covington, James W. "The Armed Occupation Act of 1842." *Florida Historical Quarterly* 40 (1961):41–52.
————. "An Episode in the Third Seminole War." *Florida Historical Quarterly* 45 (1966):45–59.
————. "Federal and State Relations with the Florida Seminoles, 1875–1901." *Tequesta* 32 (1972):17–27.
————. "The Florida Seminoles in 1847." *Tequesta* 24 (1964):49–59.
Craig, Alan K., and McJunkin, David. "Stranahan's: Last of the Seminole Trading Posts." *Florida Anthropologist* 24 (June 1971):45–49.
————, and Peebles, Christopher. "Ethnoecologic Change among the Seminoles: 1740–1840." In *Geoscience and Man, V*, edited by Bob F. Perkins. Baton Rouge: Louisiana State University Press, in press.
Davis, Hilda J. "The History of Seminole Clothing and Its Multi-Colored Designs." *American Anthropologist* 52 (1955):974–80.
Densmore, Frances. "The Seminole Indian Today." *Southern Folklore Quarterly* 18 (1954):212–21.
————. "Three Parallels between the Seminole Indians and the Ancient Greeks." *The Masterkey* 25 (1951):76–78.
Dodson, Pat. "Cruise of the Minnehaha." *Florida Historical Quarterly* 50 (1972):385–413.
————. "Hamilton Disston's St. Cloud Sugar Plantation, 1887–1901." *Florida Historical Quarterly* 40 (1971):356–69.
Dorn, J. K. "Recollections of Early Miami." *Tequesta* 9 (1949):43–59.
Dovell, Junius E. "The Railroads and Public Lands of Florida, 1879–1905." *Florida Historical Quarterly* 34 (1956):238–48.
East, Omega G. "Apache Indians in Fort Marion, 1886–1887." *El Escribano*, St. Augustine Historical Society, pp. 20–38.
Fairbanks, Charles H. "Ethnohistorical Report of the Florida Indians." Presentation before the Indian Claims Commission. Dockets 73, 151. Stencil reproduction. Washington, 1957.

First Seminole Indian Baptist Church. *Souvenir Brochure, dedicatory service, May 29, 1949.* N.p., n.d. Copy in possession of the author.

Freeman, Ethel Cutler. "Culture Stability and Change among the Seminoles of Florida." In *Men and Cultures.* Gainesville, 1965.

———. "Our Unique Indians, the Seminoles of Florida." *The American Indian* 2 (1944–45):14–27.

———. "The Seminole Woman of the Big Cypress and Her Influence in Modern Life." *American Indigena* 4 (April 1944):123–28.

———. "We Live with the Seminoles." *American Museum of Natural History* 49 (1942):226–36.

Garbarino, Merwyn S. "Seminole Girl." *Trans-Action* 7 (February 1970): 40–46.

Gifford, John C. "Five Plants Essential to the Indians and Early Settlers of Florida." *Tequesta* 4 (1944):36–44.

Gilpin, Mrs. John R. "To Miami, 1890 Style." *Tequesta* 1 (1940):89–102.

Goggin, John M. "A Florida Indian Trading Post, Circa 1763–1784." *Southern Indian Studies* 1 (1949):35–38.

———. "Florida's Indians." University of Florida *Economic Leaflets* 10 (July 1951).

———. "The Present Condition of the Florida Seminoles." *New Mexico Anthropologist* 1 (1937):37–39.

———. "Silver Work of the Florida Seminole." *El Palacio* 47 (February 1940):25–32.

———. "Source Materials for the Study of the Florida Seminoles." Laboratory Notes, Anthropology Laboratory, no. 3. University of Florida, 1959.

Greenlee, Robert F. "Aspects of Social Organization and Material Culture of the Seminole of Big Cypress Swamp." *Florida Anthropologist* 5 (December 1952):25–31.

———. "Ceremonial Practices of the Modern Seminoles." *Tequesta* 3 (1942): 25–33.

———. "Medicine and Curing Practices of the Modern Florida Seminoles." *American Anthropologist* 46 (1944):317–28.

Harrington, M. R. "Reminiscences of an Archeologist: V." *The Masterkey* 38 (January–March 1964):26–34.

———. "Seminole Adventure." *The Masterkey* 20 (1946):157–59.

———. "Seminole Oranges." *The Masterkey* 20 (1946):112.

———. "Seminole Surgeon." *The Masterkey* 27 (1953):122.

Henderson, J. R. "The Seminoles of Florida." *Wide World* (March 1926): 348–51.

Hough, Walter. "Seminoles of the Florida Swamps." *Home Geographic Monthly* 2 (1932):7–12.

Hudson, F. M. "Beginnings of Dade County." *Tequesta* 1 (1943):1–35.

Huston, W. "Los Indios Seminolas." *Revista Geographica Espanola* 7 (1940): 49–58.

Kersey, Harry A., Jr. "The Ahfachkee Day School." *Teachers College Record* 72 (September 1970): 93–103.

———. "Educating the Seminole Indians of Florida, 1879–1970." *Florida Historical Quarterly* 49 (July 1970):16–35.

———. "Pelts, Plumes and Hides: White Traders among the Seminole Indians, 1890–1930." *Florida Historical Quarterly* 52 (January 1973):250–66.

———, and Donald E. Pullease. "Bishop William Crane Gray's Mission to the Seminole Indians in Florida, 1893–1914." *Historical Magazine of the Protestant Episcopal Church* 42 (September 1973): 257–73.

MacCauley, Clay. "The Seminole Indians of Florida." Smithsonian Institution, Bureau of American Ethnology, Fifth Annual Report, 1883–1884. Washington, 1887.

Munroe, Kirk. "Alligator Hunting with Seminoles." Cosmopolitan 13 (1892): 576–81.

———. "A Forgotten Remnant." Scribner's 7 (1893):303–17.

Nash, Roy. "Survey of the Seminole Indians of Florida." Senate Doc. 314, 71st Cong., 1st sess., 1931.

Ober, Frederick A. "Ten Days with the Seminoles." Appleton's Journal of Literature, Science, and Art 14, nos. 332, 333 (July–August 1875):142–44, 171–73.

Peoples, Morgan Dewey, and Davis, Edwin Adams, eds. "Across South Central Florida in 1882: the Account of the First New Orleans Times-Democrat Exploring Expedition." Tequesta 10–11 (1950–51):49–88, 63–92.

Porter, Kenneth W. "Billy Bowlegs (Holata Micco) in the Seminole Wars (Part I)." Florida Historical Quarterly 45 (January 1967):219–42.

Protestant Episcopal Church. "Address of the Bishop." Journal of the Second Annual Convocation of the Church in the Missionary Jurisdiction of Southern Florida, 1894.

———. "Bishop's Journal." Journal of the Fifth Annual Convocation of the Church in the Missionary Jurisdiction of Southern Florida, 1897.

———. Fifteenth Annual Report of the Southern Florida Branch of the Women's Auxiliary to the Board of Missions. 1908.

Seley, Ray B., Jr. "Lieutenant Hartsuff and the Banana Plants." Tequesta 23 (1963):3–14.

Skinner, Alason B. "The Florida Seminoles." Southern Workman 40, no. 3 (1911):154–63.

———. "Notes on the Florida Seminole." American Anthropologist 15 (1913): 63–67.

Sleight, Frederick W. "Kunti: A Food Staple of the Florida Indians." Florida Anthropologist 6 (1953):46–52.

Small, John Kunkel. "Seminole Bread–The Conti: A History of the Genus Zamia in Florida." Journal of the N.Y. Botanical Garden 22, no. 259 (1921): 212–37.

Spoehr, Alexander. "Camp, Clan and Kin among the Cow Creek Seminoles of Florida." Field Museum of Natural History, Anthropological Series 33, no. 1. Chicago, 1941.

———. "The Florida Seminole Camp." Field Museum of Natural History, Anthropological Series 33, no. 3. Chicago, 1944.

Sturtevant, William C. "Accomplishments and Opportunities in Florida Indian Ethnology." In Florida Anthropology, edited by Charles H. Fairbanks. Florida Anthropological Society, Publication no. 4. Tallahassee, 1958.

———. "The Medicine Bundles and Busks of the Florida Seminoles." Florida Anthropologist 7 (May 1954):31–70.

———, ed. "R. H. Pratt's Report on the Seminole in 1879." Florida Anthropologist 9 (1956):1–24.

———. "A Seminole Personal Document." Tequesta 16 (1956):55–75.

Swanton, John R. "Early History of the Creek Indians and Their Neighbors." Smithsonian Institution, Bureau of American Ethnology, 42d Annual Report, 1924–1925. Washington, 1928.

———. "Social Organization and Social Usages of the Indians of the Creek Confederacy." Smithsonian Institution, Bureau of American Ethnology, 42d Annual Report, 1924–1925. Washington, 1928.

Utz, Dora Doster. "Life on the Loxahatchee." *Tequesta* 32 (1972):38–57.
Voss, Gilbert. "The Orange Grove House of Refuge No. 3." *Tequesta* 28 (1968):3–17.
Wagner, Henry J. "Early Pioneers of South Florida." *Tequesta* 9 (1949):61–72.
Wintringham, Mary K., ed. "North to South through the Glades in 1883; the Account of the First New Orleans *Times-Democrat* Exploring Expedition." *Tequesta* 23–24 (1963–64):33–93.

PUBLIC DOCUMENTS

Florida. *Acts,* 1899, 1935.
———. *Statutes,* 1918.
U.S. Department of the Interior. *Narrative Reports of the Superintendents of the Florida Seminole Agency and Special Commissioners, 1893–1940.* Copies of these reports are available at the University of Florida Indian Oral History Archives, Florida State Museum, Gainesville.
———, Office of Indian Affairs. Correspondence Received File (Seminole; Florida Indians), 1885–1940. Indian Oral History Archives, P. K. Yonge Library of Florida History, University of Florida, Gainesville, Florida.
U.S. House of Representatives. *Report of the Commissioner of Indian Affairs,* Exec. Doc. 1, 42d Cong., 3d sess., 1872.
———. *Report of the Commissioner of Indian Affairs.* Exec. Doc. 1, 50th Cong., 2d sess., 1888.
———. *Report of the Commissioner of Indian Affairs.* Exec. Doc. 1, 53d Cong., 2d sess., 1893.
———. *Report of the Commissioner of Indian Affairs.* Exec. Doc. 5, 55th Cong., 2d sess., 1897.
———. *Report of the Secretary of War.* Exec. Doc. 2, 35th Cong., 2d sess., 1858.
U.S. Senate. *Everglades of Florida. Acts, reports, and other papers, state and national, relating to the Everglades of the State of Florida and their reclamation.* Senate Doc. 89, 62d Cong., 1st sess., 1911.
———. *Message from the President of the United States Transmitting a Letter of the Secretary of the Interior Relative to Land upon Which to Locate Seminole Indians.* Exec. Doc. 139, 50th Cong., 1st sess., 1888.
———. *Report of the Secretary of the Interior.* Exec. Doc. 35, 40th Cong., 3d sess., 1869.
———. *Seminole Indians in Florida.* Senate Doc. 42, 63d Cong., 1st sess., 1913.
———. *Special Report of the Florida Seminole Agency.* Senate Doc. 102, 67th Cong., 2d sess., 1921.

NEWSPAPERS AND PERIODICALS

Fort Lauderdale News, 1953, 1956, 1968.
Fort Myers Daily Press, 1909–14.
Fort Myers Press, 1885–1908.
Miami Herald, 1967.
Miami Metropolis, 1907.
Palm Beach Post, 1962.
Palm Branch, 1893–1915.
St. Lucie County Tribune, 1907.
St. Petersburg Daily News, 1927.

Stuart News, 1964.
Tampa Tribune, 1959.

UNPUBLISHED MATERIALS

"Abstract of Title, Mrs. Hagen (or Rebecca Egan) Donation, January 16, 1907." Copy in files of Historical Association of Southern Florida, Miami.
"The Brown Family Papers," In possession of Mr. Percy Brown, Immokalee, Florida.
Carr, Robert. "The Brickell Store and Seminole Trade." Typescript. Tallahassee, 1974.
Copeland, D. Graham. "Data Relative to Florida," 3 vols. 1947. Typescript in the office of the Clerk of the Circuit Court, Collier County Court House, East Naples, Florida.
Day, Joseph H. "Diary of a Trip to Miami in 1877." Copy in files of Historical Association of Southern Florida, Miami.
Dedication Brochure, Collier County Court House, East Naples, 1962.
Glenn, James L. "My Work among the Florida Seminoles." Typescript in the Stranahan Papers, Historical Society of Fort Lauderdale, Florida.
"A History of the Walter Kitching and J. E. Taylor, Sr., families." Typescript. University of Florida Indian Oral History Archives, Florida State Museum, Gainesville.
"Interview with J. D. Girtman, December 10, 1938." Typescript. Florida Collection, University of South Florida Library, Tampa, Florida.
Jorgensen, Niels W. "History of White City." Typescript. St. Lucie County Museum, Fort Pierce, Florida.
Ledgers of L. M. Raulerson & Co., 1912–20. Ledger in the Special Collection, Florida Atlantic University Library, Boca Raton, Florida.
Ledgers of the Smallwood Store, Chokoloskee, Florida. The author was able to view these ledgers briefly in 1972. However, the Smallwood family has not made these materials available for scholarly research.
Ledgers of Stranahan & Company, 1906–12. Historical Society of Fort Lauderdale, Florida.
Ledgers of Walter Kitching & Co., 1914–17. In possession of Mrs. J. E. Taylor, Sr., Stuart, Florida.
Ledgers of W. B. Brickell. In possession of Mr. Stanley Cooper, Miami.
Lee County School Board. "Minutes, 1891–1908." Record books in the office of the Superintendent of Schools, Lee County Court House, Fort Myers, Florida.
MacCauley, Clay. "Inhabitants in Miami River Settlement, in the County of Dade, State of Florida, Enumerated by Me On The 9th Day of February, 1880." Copy in files of Historical Association of Southern Florida, Miami.
"Manuscript: The Brickell Family." Handwritten manuscript in the files of the *Miami Herald*. Unsigned, undated.
Meyer, Jessie H. "Development of Technical-Vocational Education at the Carlisle Indian Industrial School." Master's thesis, University of Florida, 1954.
Nicholas, James C. "The Economics of the Indian Trade in Florida." Department of Economics, Florida Atlantic University, 1973.
Post Office Information from the National Archives, Dade County, Florida, p. 30. Copy in files of Historical Association of Southern Florida, Miami.
"Reminiscences of Mrs. A. C. Richards, 1903." Collection of papers in possession of Mrs. Arva Parks, Coral Gables, Florida.

Spencer, Lucien A. "Census of the Florida Seminole Indians of Miami Agency, Fla. on June 30, 1917." Typescript in the files of the Seminole Agency, Hollywood, Florida.

———. "Census of the Seminoles in Florida as of June 30, 1973." Typescript in the files of the Seminole Agency, Hollywood, Florida.

"The Stranahan Papers." Historical Society of Fort Lauderdale, Florida.

INTERVIEWS

Tapes and transcripts of these interviews are located in the University of Florida Indian Oral History Archives, Florida State Museum, Gainesville.

Brown, W. Frank. Immokalee, Sept. 24, 1971.
Cobb, Annie. Fort Pierce, Feb. 8, 1973.
House, Mr. and Mrs. Dan. Naples, July 8, 1972.
Jorgensen, Niels W. Fort Pierce, Feb. 8, 1973.
Kennon, Rose Brown. Fort Myers, Sept. 24, 1971.
Lyman, Ralph. Lantana, Oct. 25, 1972.
McGehee, Ruby Bowers. Jupiter, Nov. 15, 1972.
Meserve, Mr. and Mrs. Ellis. Okeechobee, July 28, 1972.
Raulerson, Mr. and Mrs. Hiram. Okeechobee, July 28, 1972.
Roberts, W. D. Immokalee, Aug. 13, 1972.
Storter, Kirby. Miami, Sept. 15, 1971.
Taylor, Mrs. J. E., Sr. Stuart, Dec. 13, 1972.
Whitten, G. E. Miami, Oct. 8, 1972.

Index

151

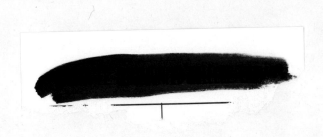